CAPITAL FORMATION AND FOREIGN INVESTMENT
IN UNDERDEVELOPED AREAS

CAPITAL FORMATION &
FOREIGN INVESTMENT
IN UNDERDEVELOPED AREAS

*An analysis of research needs and program
possibilities prepared from a study supported
by the Ford Foundation.*

CHARLES WOLF, JR.

SIDNEY C. SUFRIN

SYRACUSE
UNIVERSITY
PRESS

MAXWELL SCHOOL SERIES

SYRACUSE UNIVERSITY PRESS–1958

© 1955, 1958, Syracuse University Press

Revised, 1958

Library of Congress Catalog Card No.: 58-10620

Printed in the United States of America

To the memory of

A. S. J. B.

ACKNOWLEDGEMENTS

In PREPARING THIS REPORT, the authors acknowledge debts to many. More than one hundred and twenty scholars took time to answer the questionnaire (see page 132) which we sent them. Over sixty people participated with the authors in direct discussions of the problems dealt with in this report. Among the many who helped we particularly acknowledge the assistance of the following: Professors Everett Hagen, Wilfred Malenbaum and Max Millikan, of the Massachusetts Institute of Technology, Professor Wassily Leontief of Harvard, Professor Chandler Morse of Cornell, Professor David Riesman of Harvard University, William Turnage of the Department of State, Harold Barnett of Resources for the Future, Edward Bernstein of the International Monetary Fund, Professors Jesse Burkhead, Robert Dickinson, Preston E. James, Melvin Eggers, Frederick Mosher and A. M. McIsaac of Syracuse University, and Professor Edward Stainbrook of the Medical College of the State of New York. Where particular ideas referred to in the report were advanced by individuals in interviews or in reply to the questionnaire, an acknowledgement is made in the text.

Special thanks are due to the bibliographical and research assistance which we received from Mr. Elias Zughaib of Syracuse University and Miss Joanne MacMichael, now at the New York University Law School.

The Ford Foundation provided the funds which made this report possible. We are also indebted to the Foundation for the administrative and substantive help which they gave us. However, the conclusions, opinions and other statements in this publication are those of the authors and not necessarily those of the Ford Foundation. Cleon Swayzee, Edwin Arnold, Paul Parker and Howard Tolley, of the Foundation staff, deserve our special thanks for their continuing interest and advice. As its form and style indicate, this report was originally prepared as a working paper for informal office comment and discussion. Its publication has been undertaken with the thought that it may be of some interest to the rapidly growing number of people concerned with the problems which it discusses.

In the reprinting of the study, new bibliographic material has been added to the original select bibliographies. The kindness of Elias Zughaib, Karl Vogt, and Samuel Paul in assisting in the preparation of these bibliographic additions is appreciated. Thanks are also due to Mrs. Marjorie Hald and Frederick T. Moore for permission to use portions of a detailed bibliography on economic development and foreign aid which they prepared for The RAND Corporation.

Also added in the second printing are Appendices Three and Four, essays dealing with institutional aspects of development, and science and technology. We wish to express our appreciation to the *American Economic Review* for permission to reprint the article on "Institutions and Economic Development" (Wolf) as Appendix Three, and to the College of Business Administration of Syracuse University for permission to reprint the article on "Science and Development" (Sufrin) as Appendix Four.

We wish to express our thanks to Chancellor William P. Tolley, of Syracuse University, for his interest and assistance in the publication of this study.

The authors are, of course, alone responsible for any errors of fact or interpretation, and for the judgments advanced in the section of the report which presents recommendations.

CHARLES WOLF, JR.
SIDNEY C. SUFRIN

CONTENTS

PART ONE

INTRODUCTION

CHAPTER ONE

BACKGROUND OF THE REPORT

THE ECONOMIC DEVELOPMENT of underdeveloped areas is, as Kenneth Boulding recently observed, "the greatest single economic problem facing the world today." It is a problem whose ramifications and complexities are as great as its importance. At the same time, it is a problem on which professional economists are perhaps least sure not only of solutions, but of the adequacy of traditional methodology for uncovering them.

Despite the inadequacy of present concepts and theory, the scale of effort currently being devoted to problems of development and capital formation is considerable. The program activities of many of the underdeveloped countries, together with assistance from the United Nations and its specialized agencies, the International Bank, the United States Foreign Operations Administration, and agencies of the British Commonwealth and other economically advanced nations, suggest that historians may regard economic development in the 20th century as another example of the maxim that policy and action frequently precede the elaboration of satisfactory theory.

At the same time as program activities are expanding, research on problems of development has been growing apace. In the United States alone at least a dozen major universities are engaged in studies and projects having a direct bearing on problems of development, in addition to the relevant studies being undertaken by government agencies and by such private groups as the Committee for Economic Development and the National Planning Association. Ideally, there should be a close and reciprocal relation between research and program efforts in this general field: research in one period providing the foundation for subsequent program activity; and program experience in one period uncovering problems and data for subsequent research. That this relationship is as infrequent in practice as it is desirable in principle is one reason behind this study.

The present study was undertaken a) to prepare a partial inventory of research already under way or recently completed dealing with capital formation and foreign investment in underdeveloped areas; and b) to use this inventory as a basis for an analysis and evaluation of additional research needs and possibilities for applying, through action programs, the results or ideas derived from recent research in this field. Although the general concern of the authors has been with economic development broadly, an effort was made at the outset to concentrate on indigenous capital formation as a critical variable in economic growth, and on foreign investment as a possible "trigger" for indigenous investment.

Several points bearing on this approach, and the subject matter in general, should be noted at the outset:

First: capital formation is but one aspect of economic development and not necessarily the causal one. Though reasoning by historical analogy is not conclusive, the industrial revolution in the West was probably not initiated by a rapid expansion of investment. Rather, investment grew as a concomitant of the inventions and innovations, which jointly launched the Industrial (and Agricultural) Revolution. Realistically, an increased rate of capital formation is a necessary aspect of economic development;[1] it is not a sufficient explanation or cause.[2]

Second: in identifying and evaluating the strategic points to which pressure should be applied to accelerate economic growth *and* capital formation, the enquiry must be extended beyond the familiar categories of economic analysis. In a sense, there is hardly any branch of social science whose subject matter does not have some bearing on problems of growth and investment in underdeveloped areas.

---

[1]Theoretically, development could be achieved and sustained without any increase in capital stock by continued changes in technology and productivity. In practice, increased capital formation and improved technology are likely to be interconnected and mutually reenforcing.

[2]Dr. Kuznets has raised a different question concerning the causal role frequently assigned to capital formation in economic development.

> "If certain elements in consumption are strategic in increasing labor's productivity, and it is thus possible to secure higher rates of growth by increasing consumption (and reducing capital formation) as a proportion of national product, is it desirable to maintain a distinction between consumption and capital formation as means of increasing labor productivity?" in *A Survey of Contemporary Economics,* vol. II, B. F. Haley, editor, Homewood, Illinois, 1952, p. 180.

His point that increased consumption may sometimes have as significant an impact on productivity as increased "investment," though perhaps a special case, suggests the kind of terminological problems sometimes encountered in applying standard economic categories to problems of development.

Summarizing the status of contemporary economic thought on the subject of development and capital formation, Professor Abramowitz noted:

> The foundation of an adequate theory of capital formation does, in fact, involve grappling with a complex sociological tangle which can hardly be unraveled with the aid of such concepts and hypotheses as economics now furnishes. . .
>
> The economics of growth is, therefore, the field of work in which the dependence of economics upon its sister social sciences appears in a supreme degree.[3]

Ragnar Nurkse concludes his recent book on capital formation in underdeveloped countries with a similar, if milder, statement:

> We have reached a field of sociological rather than economic considerations, and at the border of this field I will stop. That we have come to it is not surprising, for the advancement of the underdeveloped countries is far more than an economic problem.[4]

Third: realization of the relevance of non-economic factors may lead to such undisciplined speculation about human motivation and social variability as to be fruitless from the standpoint of suggesting either workable action programs or significant research hypotheses.[5]

In the light of these considerations, we have tried to frame our analysis of capital formation and foreign investment in relation to those problem areas which seem to offer the greatest untried opportunities for immediate or potential *program application*.

On the research side, we have especially tried to identify what might be called areas of "program" research, i.e., research directed toward those questions which seem to have direct implications for economic development programming, especially in the countries of South and Southeast Asia and the Near East.

In developing the inventory of current and recently completed research, three methods of enquiry were relied upon: (1) A questionnaire was sent to 200 individuals and institutions in the United States and Canada, Latin America, Europe, and, through the Ford Foundation field representatives, in the Near East and South and Southeast Asia. The questionnaire was pre-

---

[3]Abramowitz, Moses, "The Economics of Growth," in *A Survey of Contemporary Economics*, ibid., pp. 161-162, 177.

[4]Nurkse, Ragnar, *Problems of Capital Formation in Underdeveloped Countries*, New York, 1953, p. 157.

[5]In this connection it might be noted that the interdisciplinary activity and interest stimulated by consideration of economic development problems is one of the most interesting, and may be one of the most important, developments in current social science. Of several attempts which have been made to develop an "interdisciplinary" conceptual framework, at least in broad outline, for analyzing economic development problems, those of Professor W. W. Rostow and Professor E. P. Reubens might be singled out. (See Reubens, E. P. *American Economic Review*, May 1953, pp. 126-130, and Rostow, W. W., *The Process of Economic Growth*, New York, 1953.)

pared as a check list of research topics designed to elicit from the respondent information concerning his research in this field. An analysis of the 127
responses received and a copy of the questionnaire are attached as Appendix One; (2) Conversations were held with over sixty people in government, business and in academic institutions in the United States who have
studied various aspects of capital formation in underdeveloped areas. A
summary and analysis of these conversations is included as Appendix Two;
(3) A review of some four hundred books, periodicals and other recently
published materials was conducted with the assistance of Miss Joann Mac-
Michael, working at the Library of Congress, and Mr. Elias Zughaib at
Syracuse University. Selected titles from this review, together with brief
descriptive comments, comprise the bibliography (Chapter Six) of this
Report. A separate section of the bibliography describes briefly a number
of current research projects in the United States and abroad dealing with
investment problems in underdeveloped areas.

In assembling the bibliography, we have in general restricted our review of published research to the years since 1949.[6] Of the published material we have made a further selection as to what has seemed to us most
relevant to our enquiry. In selecting material, we have tried to consider
what would be especially relevant to the problems of capital formation in
South and Southeast Asia and the Near East; but, in general, our attention
has been directed toward material dealing with function and process more
broadly, rather than with unique elements of a particular country situation. However, studies of particular countries have in some instances been
included for their intrinsic as well as suggestive value. Clearly, in the subsequent application of findings in this report, especially those relating to
program, variations in individual country situations may be of decisive
importance.

An analysis purporting to deal with the "underdeveloped areas," as
such, plainly runs the risk of assuming a homogeneity among those areas
which does not invariably exist. Empty generalizations may result. At the
other extreme is the danger of excessive particularization which may obscure points of general applicability to more than one country. In dealing
with the material in this study, we have tried to avoid both extremes by
considering general ideas and approaches in relation to the regions of the
Near East, and South and Southeast Asia. The recommendations and conclusions reached can be further developed and tested by a comparative

[6]This study was begun in October 1953, and a first draft was completed by March 1954.
Professor Wolf devoted full-time, and Professor Sufrin part-time, to the study during
this period. Further work was done by both authors in the summer of 1954 to put
the report in its final form.

analysis of different socio-economic regions. Such an analysis is not, however, attempted in this study.

In sending the questionnaires, we have no doubt inadvertently overlooked individuals and institutions inside and outside the United States who are working on some aspects of the broad problems of capital formation and foreign investment in underdeveloped areas. Moreover, when responses have not been received, we have had to assume that there was no relevant research to report. In some instances responses consisted of advice to communicate with other individuals or institutions. In most cases this has been done. For these and other reasons, the inventory contained in Chapter Six is partial and selective. Notwithstanding these limitations, it is hoped that the inventory will be of interest and use, both to scholars and administrators interested in investment problems in underdeveloped areas, as a suggestive guide to approaches currently being considered.

The analysis and findings in Part Two are essentially reflections and judgements evolving from the process of "research on research" described above. The findings try to highlight certain needs for additional research and possibilities for program action, which are perhaps inadequately recognized, but which seem to the authors to be most promising from the standpoint of increasing the quantity of investment in the underdeveloped areas and directing it toward fields of maximum productivity. Part Two is not an exercise in theory or model-building. Instead, it attempts to block out three main problem areas and, within each, to analyze the problem briefly and suggest some specific research needs and program possibilities. These problem areas are: (1) *Entrepreneurship and the Demand for Capital;* (2) *Technological Alternatives and the Optimum Use of Capital;* (3) *Foreign Investment and Capital Formation.* Throughout the discussion, an effort has been made to relate these problems to research by individuals and institutions working on them.

While these problem areas have seemed to the authors to be the most fruitful, in terms of suggesting present program possibilities or research needs likely to yield new program conclusions, they clearly do not exhaust the field. A fourth section has been included to present some of the additional areas in which definable research needs and program possibilities exist.

A few observations on the terminology used in the study should be noted. "Economic growth" and "economic development" are used interchangeably to mean increased real per capita output. The term "capital" is used to denote real production facilities, including not only tools, machinery, transport facilities, plant and equipment, but such additional forms of capital, (which are frequently of particular importance in agricultural economies), as value added by clearing land, and new plantings of crops

with long-growth periods.[7] The term productive or "active" capital is used
to distinguish such capital which directly leads to additional employment
and/or output in subsequent periods,[8] from "passive" capital which lacks
these effects, or at least does not have them to the same extent. The ratio
between the value of capital formation and the discounted present value
of the increased output to which it leads is lower for active than passive
capital.

A large volume of underemployed or unemployed resources, especially
labor, often characterizes the underdeveloped areas. Active capital helps to
put these resources to work. Under such circumstances, investments with a
low ratio of capital to output may normally be assumed to have priority
over investments with a higher capital-output ratio. This distinction may
be difficult to apply. Its applicability may, for example, vary with the accounting or planning period considered. Frequently, what is apparently
passive or unproductive capital is highly necessary in any given economic
structure as a "social overhead" input, which, by reducing costs for the individual enterprise, stimulates subsequent inputs of more directly productive investment and so raises output over the long run. It is thus true that
certain kinds of investment, which might be considered unproductive or
passive in the short run, such as roads, irrigation dams, railroads, etc., are
highly productive in the longer-run.[9] Notwithstanding such difficulties in
the definition, measurement and use of capital-output ratios, the distinction between active and passive capital has significance for discussing
investment problems in underdeveloped areas, as we will try to show.

[7]In a sense, increased labor skill, through training and education, can have a similar
effect on output as an increase in the stock of capital. For this reason, some writers
have referred to an economy's technology as its "invisible capital." Although attention
is given in this study to the relationship between technological change and capital
formation, the two are conceptually distinct.
[8]Assuming that market conditions are favorable.
[9]There are other technical difficulties connected with a too-mechanical use of the
capital-output ratio in approximating what we mean by "active" capital. The difference
between the services of capital entering into output, and the value of the output itself,
generally represents the contribution of other factors of production. It is at least possible that some of these factors may be scarcer and more expensive than capital. In
such cases, investments having a higher capital-output ratio may be preferable to those
having a lower ratio. However, other things being equal, low capital-output ratios are
indicative of active capital if the other factors entering into output are abundant and
cheap. Another difficulty arises from the fact that the capital-output ratio may simply
depend on the stage of production considered in making the calculation. If the calculation is made closer to the retail stage, the ratio is likely to be lower because the value
of total output will be high though value-added may be low.
For these reasons, the distinction between "active" and "passive" capital in the text
involves more than the notion of capital-output ratios. It involves particularly the notion of a generative effect on new output which some investments are and others are
not likely to have. Clearly, more work needs to be done to determine precisely what
kinds of investments are likely to play such an active role in particular socio-economic
situations. The present report presents this issue but does not resolve it.

PART TWO

ANALYSIS AND FINDINGS

CHAPTER TWO

ENTREPRENEURSHIP AND THE DEMAND FOR CAPITAL

The Problem. The traditional model of underdeveloped economies presents the problem of capital formation as a scarcity of total output and income. Given the low level of per capita real income characterizing underdeveloped economies, the model assumes that average and marginal consumption propensities are high, that savings are low and that the formation of new productive capital is therefore restricted. The low level of capital formation, in turn, sharply restricts the rate of growth in real output, and, allowing for population growth, a tendency toward static equilibrium results, with no growth in per capita real output and no tendency toward such growth. In brief, too much tends to be consumed and too little left over for investment; and this situation in turn perpetuates the initially low level of income.

Many examples can be cited to illustrate this model. In India in 1950-1, net savings were estimated at 5 per cent of national income compared with about 15 per cent in the United States. Assuming an average capital-output ratio of three to one, as suggested in the Indian Five Year Plan, and allowing for an annual rate of population growth of 1.3 per cent, it can be readily seen that real per capita income would remain nearly static.

Notwithstanding the plausibility of the foregoing model, there are good reasons for doubting—at least in enough cases to be significant—whether, in many cases, it is the shortage of total resources which restricts productive capital formation; or whether it is rather the shortage of a *key* or strategic resource which inhibits the utilization of resources that are available for investment. Stated more specifically, frequently, in underdeveloped economies, the supply of savings is a less significant limitation on the rate of productive investment than the demand for capital.

Several kinds of evidence can be cited to support this proposition. In some underdeveloped countries the accumulation of internal cash balances, through government fiscal transactions, suggests the existence of idle resources potentially available for productive capital formation. For example, during the period 1951 to mid 1953, the net cash balances of the Government of Thailand, including stabilization account deposits, rose by 1.3 billion baht (about $75 million) or 50 per cent of the government's actual outlays on development. In other cases, balance of payments surpluses, resulting in the growth of foreign exchange reserves, imply the existence of "savings" realized by the economy as a whole which could be used to increase productive investment. The familiar assumption that newly developing countries characteristically tend to incur balance of payments deficits is not always valid. Frequently they tend to "overcontrol" imports and to accumulate exchange reserves in the process. In this connection, India's recent payments surpluses, though not large, assume a greater significance when viewed in terms of the intention expressed in the Five Year Plan to draw down the country's sterling balances at an annual rate of 35 million. Moreover, the frequent tendency of the international accounts of underdeveloped countries to be characterized by an outward movement of capital, and for the private funds of wealthy citizens of these countries to be held in banks and securities of the United States, the United Kingdom or Switzerland, afford typical illustrations of the existence of savings which are not being used to increase productive capacity.

There are other and more impressive indications that even existing levels of savings in underdeveloped economies are not being fully used for capital formation. By an analysis of the assumed net savings ratios and the total investment targets in the Indian Five Year Plan, Wilfred Malenbaum of the Massachusetts Institute of Technology has indicated that the planned investment for development in the public sector and the organized private sector of the Indian economy, if fully realized, will only account for 55 per cent of the economy's estimated "net investible resources" (i.e. net real savings, planned utilization of sterling balances, external aid already received, and estimated private foreign investment) available over the 1951-1956 period of the Plan.[10] Although there is little information avail-

---

[10]Malenbaum, Wilfred, "The Government in Economic Development in India," Unpublished Paper, Center for International Studies, Cambridge, Mass., October 1953. The actual figures recorded for the first two years of the Plan are, in relative terms nearly identical to Malenbaum's five year estimates. Thus, using figures contained in the Five Year Plan, it can be shown that net investible resources (net savings plus foreign aid and foreign investment) available in the period 1951-1953 were estimated at about $2.3 billion in rupee equivalent. The Progress Report of the Planning Commission places actual development outlays for the two years at $1.35 billion, consisting of $1.2 billion of public sector outlays—even this level being perhaps overstated by inclusion of some gross investment outlays—and $125 million of investment by the organized private sector. Thus, development outlays for the first two years account for 58 per cent of net investible resources (See *Five Year Plan Progress Report for 1951-1952* and 1952-1953, p. 4 and p. 84 for public and private sector figures respectively).

able on the remaining 45 per cent, Malenbaum suggests that a large share of it is invested by the savers themselves and apparently goes into what we have called "passive" forms of capital.

If investments take such passive forms as residential construction, accumulation of gold or foreign exchange, or the "flight" of capital, then the quantity of active capital formation might be increased merely by a change in the pattern of investment.[11]

In addition to expanding active capital formation through the more effective use of *existing* savings in the underdeveloped countries, there are also indications that the supply of savings may be somewhat more flexible than the traditional model suggests. The recent Indian National Sample Survey, for example, has indicated that over seven per cent of rural expenditures on an all-India basis, are typically for ceremonial purposes such as celebrations, marriages, births, funerals, etc., with a regional variation ranging from four per cent in South India to nearly 16 per cent in West India. An additional six per cent, as a national average, is spent on tobacco, intoxicants, refreshments and amusements. Arguments can be adduced for according such consumption a higher place on the Indian rural consumer's preference scale than the character of the consumption itself might suggest. However, it is likely that marginal adjustments in this volume of expenditure would be possible if there were an effective incentive to invest, i.e. if the demand for capital were sufficiently strong. It might be mentioned in this connection that Egbert de Vries of the International Bank and Elmer Starch, formerly with the Mutual Security Agency, commenting on their respective experiences in Indonesia and Turkey, both mentioned situations in which the *marginal* propensity to save, even in relatively poor rural areas, tended sometimes to be surprisingly high, reaching about 60 per cent in those cases where a strong local demand for capital existed. Generally, in these cases the acts of saving and investment tend to be closely related, and are frequently indistinguishable.

Another potentially major source of increased savings lies in the mobilization of the large volume of underemployed rural labor in many of the underveloped economies. Labor is potentially the richest and usually the most wasted resource in many of the underdeveloped countries. Unemployment and underemployment in India, for example, may annually waste as many gross man-years of labor as is contributed by the entire labor force

[11]Marginal productivity analysis traditionally, and operations research and programming analysis currently, recognize the importance of different kinds of capital formation in maximizing stated objectives. Aggregative economic analysis has tended to obscure the importance of different *kinds* of capital formation for two reasons: first, by concentrating on the statistical identity between savings and investment in the aggregate; and second, by assuming that the interest and (anticipated) profit rates in the market would automatically tend to guide capital into the most productive investments.

of the United States. Assuming no change in average labor productivity, the full employment of India's unemployed and underemployed might raise Indian national income by as much as 15-20 per cent.[12] In Syria, 70-80 per cent of the working population is engaged in agricultural pursuits, and disguised unemployment is estimated as high as 25-30 per cent. Thus about 20 per cent of the working population could be put to work on non-farming jobs without reducing agricultural output.[13]

Full employment of idle or underemployed labor would plainly require some additional capital for technical reasons alone. But the capital requirements might be relatively small, and the necessary redistribution of total consumption relatively slight, if the consumption of the newly employed were not to be significantly changed from current levels.

From the point of view of capital formation, the most significant effect of unemployment is to dissipate "savings" which might otherwise be available for productive investment. The individual cultivator in the typical subsistence agriculture of much of Asia and the Near East produces or can produce several times his own consumption requirements, even with present techniques.[14] Apart from the various ways in which this "surplus" is partially siphoned from the cultivator through excessive rental charges, interest rates, tolls and other levies, the bulk is dissipated by the non-producing members of the joint family, the clan or corresponding family unit. (Kinship ties are so strong in the Near East, for example, that anyone with the same surname as another may claim assistance from him.)

It is perhaps surprising that relatively little attention has been given in recent literature on economic development to the great opportunity for increasing capital formation in the underdeveloped countries by putting underemployed rural labor to work on various capital-creating projects, without any necessary "belt-tightening" in the process. Ragnar Nurkse of Columbia University has presented one of the few insightful and systematic formulations of this problem.[15] In Nurkse's model, the utilization of

---

[12]Estimated on the basis of an average productivity per employed worker of $50 and underemployment and unemployment of 60 million man-years equivalent. As used in the text, the amount of underemployment is defined as the number of workers that could be withdrawn from agricultural employment without reducing total output, given constant production functions.

[13]Sufrin, S. C. and Zughaib, E. *Political and Economic Crosscurrents in Syria.* Unpublished paper, Maxwell Research Center, Syracuse, December 1953.

[14]This generalization is frequently obscured by the tendency to "make work" and stretchout labor requirements. (The use of the *ani-ani* knife to cut each individual rice stalk separately at harvest time in Indonesia is a case in point.) In such instances, the "individual cultivator" referred to in the text may be a hypothetical construct. He becomes a reality when considered in conjunction with the definition of underemployment stated in footnote 12.

[15]Nurkse, R., op. cit., pp. 36-47.

underemployed labor depends on the mobilization of the "subsistence fund"—representing the consumption of the underemployed labor—in the village, and its channeling to the labor which is to be relocated in areas where capital-creating projects are undertaken. Actually, the problem may be somewhat simpler, since as a *program* matter, the capital-creating projects may be located in the same village areas where the underemployed labor resides. In this case, the fiscal problems of mobilizing and channeling the subsistence fund become superseded by the program problem of evoking a voluntary or semi-voluntary labor supply. The Indian Community Development Program is based in large part on this "self-help" approach. Although there is room for considerable expansion in this field, the imputed value of voluntary village labor contributed during the Program's first year has been estimated at 40 per cent of the direct financial contribution of the state governments.[16]

The objection may be raised that the problems of converting idle labor and less-essential consumption into capital, involve an increase in the *supply* of savings, and hence differ from the problem of securing a more effective use of existing savings by strengthening the *demand* for productive capital. Given the social and locational structure of many of the underdeveloped economies, this distinction is less meaningful upon second look. In the context of local and closely-knit village communities, the demand for capital—especially to the extent it is recognized and accepted by the community as its own demand—directly affects the supply of savings. Voluntary rationing operates in such communities when a common goal requires it. The mobilization of marginal increases in savings, and their redirection toward newly employed village labor, engaged in constructing capital facilities, may depend significantly on measures to strengthen the demand for capital within the local community. As Henry Aubrey noted, in discussing the role of small industry in economic development, both existing and potential savings in the village are to a considerable extent non-transferable: they will either be available for *local* capital formation, if the demand for such capital is strong enough at the local level, or they will be dissipated.[17] In a real sense, and within certain important limits, an inverse version of Say's law may apply to the supply of savings in underdeveloped economies: a sufficiently strong demand for capital may create its own supply of savings.

Up to this point we have stressed the opportunity for using *current* (and potential) net savings for productive capital formation. Theoretically, it

[16]*Kurushektra*. First Year's Report on the Community Projects, Oct. 2, 1953 New Delhi.
[17]Aubrey, H. "The Role of Small Industry in Economic Development," *Social Research* May 1951, p. 295.

should also be possible to finance an expansion of active capital in the underdeveloped countries by disinvestment of passive capital that has already been accumulated. Thus, quite apart from the point previously made that current net savings in many of the underdeveloped countries are not being effectively used, disinvestment of already accumulated capital can be considered capable of providing additional resources for productive investment. Disinvestment can provide resources for expanding new and active capital in two ways: through the sale or liquidation of some of the economy's unproductive assets, such as the gold and jewels that in some of the underdeveloped countries are used for ritualistic and decorative purposes;[18] and through allowing passive capital to depreciate without replacement, thereby freeing a corresponding part of the economy's gross current savings for the formation of active capital.

Basically, this point reduces itself to the proposition that productive investment in an underdeveloped economy can be increased through disinvestment and reinvestment of accumulated wealth, if the demand for new productive investment is sufficiently strong. However, the difficulty in mobilizing accumulated assets for new investment should be plainly admitted. The structure of a country's past, as well as its present investment, is a function of its social, cultural and religious, as well as its economic, values and motivations. The value accorded production and development in an economy must compete with other values in determining how the accumulated, as well as current, resources of that economy are used. The liquidation of assets, accumulated for "unproductive" ritualistic purposes, and the utilization of the proceeds for irrigation pumps, generators, tools, machinery, manufacturing plant, etc., involves such a major overturning of collective tradition and individual preference scales, as to raise major doubts concerning feasibility. This doubt applies as well to the changed use of current net savings as to the disinvestment of accumulated assets. Social inertia thus constitutes an important qualification to the argument we have been advancing. Yet this qualification is itself significant in highlighting an important fact, namely that the problem of capital formation in underdeveloped countries is frequently less a problem of scarce resources, in an absolute, life-sustaining sense, than it is of competing *values* —explicit and implicit—within these societies, as to the uses to which resources should be put, whether for productive capital formation or for other purposes.

---

[18]As an illustration, although there is no reliable census on the subject, quite startling guesses have been made on the value of the gold in Burma's innumerable gilded pagodas, running into hundreds of millions of dollars. The Government of Pakistan's Public Investment Enquiry Committee in 1951 estimated "hoarded wealth" in Pakistan at a value of $600-$900 million held mainly in the form of gold, silver bars and ornaments.

The foregoing discussion may be briefly summarized by the following propositions:

(1) The familiar model of underdeveloped economies represents the limitation on capital formation as stemming from an absolute shortage of total output and income, which in turn makes the restricted supply of savings the immediate factor limiting the formation of active capital.

(2) In some of the more important underdeveloped countries, however, the supply of savings is a less significant limitation on the rate of capital formation than the *demand* for productive capital.

(3) Several different kinds of evidence may be cited in support of the foregoing generalization: (a) indications that net current savings, in many underdeveloped countries and to a considerable extent, are not being fully utilized for capital formation; (b) data suggesting that, even given existing low levels of real income, savings could frequently be increased—especially through the mobilization of underemployed rural labor—*if* the demand for capital were sufficiently strong and effective; and (c) indications that the probable size of already-accumulated stocks of passive capital would permit disinvestment of a portion, (e.g. by export and sale in the case of precious metals, and by the depreciation process in the case of certain fixed investments) and the reinvestment of proceeds in more active capital.

(4) To some extent, therefore, the problem of changing the quantity of active capital in underdeveloped countries is a problem of changing the structure and pattern of current and of previous investment as well.

One qualification needs to be added to the above discussion. The argument we have been making should not be interpreted as either a denial of the pressure of poverty or the urgent need for development in the underdeveloped areas. Nor does it carry any negative implications concerning United States economic aid policy. Clearly, economic aid involves questions concerning the necessary rate of development and the realities of international political competition, which we have not touched on. Moreover, the contention, that in some of the major under-developed countries aggregate resource shortages do not presently constitute the main limitation on capital formation, is not intended to imply that aggregate resource shortages may not become a major limitation in the future. It should also be emphasized that frequently an anticipated shortage of resources for capital formation has the effect of preventing or delaying the more effective use of already-existing resources.

Nevertheless, it might be contended that when the underdeveloped countries reach a point where the rate of productive investment is so high that further expansion is prevented only by resource shortages in the aggregate, perhaps this in itself will indicate that the most fundamental problems of economic development have already been solved and a process of dynamic growth begun. The ideological and institutional elements of the society may then have been adjusted to assist development. Although additional adjustments may be required, the initial inertia would have been overcome.

If, then, resources do exist in the underdeveloped countries for increasing capital formation, the question arises whether productive and profitable opportunities for using capital exist.

Adam Smith's classical exposition of the role of limited market size in deterring investment and technological change[19] has found recent applicability to problems of underdeveloped areas. Ragnar Nurkse has reemphasized the restrictive effect of a limited domestic market on the inducement to invest, treating the small size of the market as itself fundamentally a reflection of low domestic productivity in the underdeveloped countries.[20] It is frequently also pointed out that there is not much any individual producer or investor can do to break this barrier, because of the inapplicability of Say's law at the micro-economic level: i.e. supply does not create its own demand at the level of the individual producer.

The usual policy prescriptions for breaking the barrier are (a) concentration on public utilities investment, especially in transportation and communications, as a means of widening the market and as a source of economies external to the firm which may so lower costs as to overcompensate for the initially small size of the market; and (b) a simultaneous expansion of investment on many fronts and on a sufficient scale to assist the market for individual commodities to expand at the same time as production is rising.

Although it is plausible that the limited domestic market to some extent dampens investment incentives, there are both theoretical and empirical reasons for questioning its general applicability. Theoretically, international trade provides one opportunity for an immediate widening of the market; an opportunity which may be further exploited by the use of appropriate foreign exchange and commercial policies. A country's import lists provide one indication of commodities for which there is an already established market. And any replacement of imports by domestic output creates a potential increase in the domestic market as well. Where, as is frequently the case, an underdeveloped country imports food, any increased domestic food output can normally expect to find a ready domestic market at prevailing prices unless the farmers and their families consume the in-

---

[19] ". . . division of labor must always be limited by . . . the extent of the market," Adam Smith, *The Wealth of Nations,* New York, 1933, Vol. 1, p. 15.
[20] Nurkse, *op. cit.,* pp. 7-17.

creased product. If they sell it, the income received by farmers from the increased output in turn increases their demand for products at least some of which may be produced at home or which may be temporarily imported by using the exchange freed from reduced food imports.

Exports offer a similar means of widening the limited domestic market. Investment leading to increased export raises income and effective demand, at least some of which may be directed toward products that can be produced domestically.

It is frequently maintained that international trade is not a feasible answer to the limited size of the domestic market, because there are no or few additional products which the underdeveloped countries can produce *competitively* with imports or exports on world markets. Quite apart from the merits or demerits of using commercial policy, foreign exchange policy or subsidies as special inducements to investment in import-replacing or export-expanding industries, there are, in fact, many fields in which investment and output in the underdeveloped countries *do not* automatically expand even though the *country concerned has an immediate market outlet and a demonstrable comparative advantage over competitors.* One specific example of this apparently surprising generalization will suffice; many others might be mentioned.

Among the most fertile rice land in the world is the delta of the Irrawaddy River in Burma, one of the world's largest rice exporters. Yields in this area are roughly comparable to yields in other parts of Southeast Asia. There are two problems which have prevented a substantial increase in output, quite apart from changes in cultivation techniques. The first of these has to do with the shortness of the growing (wet) season which prevents double-cropping. The second problem arises from a somewhat more complicated situation. Much of the Irrawaddy delta consists of small islands, many of them perhaps 90,000 cultivable acres. Frequently two-thirds of the area of these islands comprise lowlands, which are uncultivated throughout the year because of inundation during the monsoon, and an accumulation of brackish, stagnant water during the dry season. Farming in one season of the year is restricted to a relatively narrow strip around the edge of the island. It is a fairly simple and relatively inexpensive matter to install a small steel sluice gate and a concrete runway, with distributive dirt channels, at the head of the island, thereby permitting the controlled inflow of silted river water to build up the low center basin of the island. Under the recent U.S. assistance program in Burma, a number of projects of this kind have been activated. Installed at an average total foreign exchange and local cost of $100,000 such a gate and runway add about 750 acre-feet of silt per year and permit the reclamation of over 300 acres for cultivation annually. At an average yield of about two-thirds ton per acre per crop, and an average export price of perhaps $140 per ton, the total original investment would be amortized in less than six years.[21]

This example is typical of the highly profitable opportunities existing in many of the underdeveloped economies for the use of relatively small amounts of capital *within the framework of the current market situation* faced by these countries. Nor is technology the bottleneck in the strict sense of that term. The analysis and engineering required for this kind of small scale reclamation was completed by the British and known generally in Burma well before World War II. Granted the less favorable market situation at that time, it is still probable that a strong profit incentive for raising productivity did exist. An explanation for the failure to take advantage of this situation must go beyond economic considerations.

There is also some question whether limited market size has, historically, been as strong a deterrent to new investment as Nurkse's observations would imply. In the development of Soviet Russia and Japan, it is true that simultaneous expansion of investment on many fronts was enforced, and hence a solution to the market problem, in a sense, was "built-in" to the method of development. In Western development, however, it is questionable whether the wave of investment stimulated by such innovations as the printing press, the cotton gin, and the railroad were significantly deterred by the limited size of the original market. Instead, both the functioning of international trade and the displacement of other products from a given national bill of goods, in what Professor Schumpeter aptly termed "the process of creative destruction," provided means for surmounting the apparent obstacle of limited market size.

The foregoing is not intended to imply that limited market size is not a factor influencing the direction and strength of inducements to invest. Rather it is intended to support the contention that, notwithstanding the existence of a limited domestic market in the underdeveloped areas, there are, typically, many highly attractive investment opportunities which remain unexploited.

If, then, resources for increasing capital formation exist within many of the underdeveloped countries, and if at the same time untried oppor-

[21]Of the total costs of the project, aside from the steel gate and concrete runway, the bulk represents the cost of labor, which is otherwise unemployed during the dry season when the construction is undertaken. Such complicating factors as the controlled internal price of rice, distribution costs from farm to port, et cetera, are purposely excluded. Quantitatively these negative factors would be more than offset by an extension of the benefits from the project described in the text by using the same capital facilities for drainage and irrigation. For further details, see Wolf, C., *Selected Economic Development Projects in Burma and Indonesia,* Cornell University, Southeast Asia Program, Data Paper No. 15, August 1954, Ithaca, New York. Since this description was written, the international market for rice has deteriorated. Consequently, the other projects cited in the Cornell Data paper provide better illustrations of the point suggested in the text.

tunities for the profitable and productive use of capital also, typically, exist, a fundamental question, which an inquiry into the problem of capital formation must answer, is: Why doesn't an acceleration in productive investment take place automatically?

The economist's answer to this question is usually phrased in terms of "imperfections in the market." The sociologist's answer is usually phrased in terms of social structure and the need for a change from "particularistic" to "universalistic" relationships if economic incentives are to become effective.[22] To follow the terminology we have been using, the answer might be formulated as follows: The rate of productive capital formation in underdeveloped economies is frequently inhibited not by a shortage of resources in the aggregate, or by a lack of profitable opportunities for the use of capital, but rather by the shortage of a *particular key or strategic resource:* entrepreneurship, the function of perceiving and effectuating new combinations of factors of production in order to take advantage of existing or anticipated market situations.[23] Following Schumpeter's definition of entrepreneur, we shall consider him as the creative business leader, who, with the help of credit and technology, innovates or creatively applies unused or new techniques and ideas to the economic process. "For actions which consist in carrying out innovations we reserve the term Enterprise, the individuals who carry them out we call Entrepreneurs."[24] The entrepreneur *may* supply capital, but his prime function is to supply innovation—his own original ideas or borrowed ideas. The point is he dares to do something in a way it has not generally been done.

The entrepreneurial function constitutes the essential link required to bring available resources and existing investment opportunities together. The lack of this link retards potential demand for productive capital in many of the underdeveloped economies.

This formulation is, essentially, consistent with the two formulations previously cited. The lack of entrepreneurship is, in effect, responsible for the "market imperfection" which accounts for factor immobilities, and more specifically, for the flow of savings into passive rather than active

[22]cf. Levy, Marion J. "Contrasting Factors in the Modernization of China and Japan," *Economic Development and Cultural Change,* October 1953, and "Some Sources of the Vulnerability of the Structures of Relatively Non-Industrialized Societies to Those of Highly Industrialized Societies," in *The Progress of Underdeveloped Areas,* (Hoselitz, B. F., ed.) Chicago, 1952, pp. 116-117.
[23]Schumpeter, J. "Economic Theory and Entrepreneurial History" in *Change and the Entrepreneur,* p. 68 ff. For our present purposes, no attempt is made to refine this definition by a subdivision of the different types and degrees of entrepreneurship. As used in the text, the term primarily refers to the "innovating" and "imitative" types of entrepreneurship as these categories are defined by Professor Danhof and reported in *Change and the Entrepreneur,* Cambridge, 1949, pp. 23-24.
[24]Schumpeter, J. *Business Cycles*—New York, 1939, p. 102.

uses[25] in the underdeveloped economies. At the same time, the lack of entrepreneurship is, fundamentally, a symptom of a particular social structure characterizing underdeveloped areas: a social structure which places a premium on what one economist has termed the "use of resources to maintain status rather than to increase production."

It should be noted that the above formulation of the problem of capital formation makes no distinction between the exercise of entrepreneurship by public authorities and private individuals. The history of past development experience shows a variety of different and changing combinations between public and private entrepreneurship in the process of growth. Between the poles of preponderant private entrepreneurship in U.S. development and exclusively state entrepreneurship in the Soviet Union, the experience of Japan and Sweden suggest that other combinations have been feasible and successful.[26]

The developmental problems of the Near East and South and Southeast Asia are so vast that more than a single type of entrepreneurial initiative is necessary. In practice the use of both public and private entrepreneurship, and various possible combinations of the two, may not raise the same ideological issues in the East which are usually associated with it in the West. In discharging its already recognized responsibilities for providing social overhead capital, government entrepreneurship is likely to be fully absorbed for the next decade or more, given the present character and orientation of government in the Near Eastern and Asian areas. The expansion of active capital in other fields is likely to require the increasing development of private entrepreneurship because of the organizational and administrative limitations under which new governments will be operating.

The suggestion that entrepreneurship is the key resource, whose lack impedes capital formation in many underdeveloped countries, raises a series of questions concerning the barriers to entrepreneurship. At the same time, this formulation suggests that greater analytical attention should be devoted to appraising these barriers and devising program

---

[25]In making this distinction, we are aware of the classical explanation of passive capital accumulation as motivated by "place" and "time" utilities. To a considerable extent, place and time utilities can be used as an explanation for passive capital accumulation in underdeveloped areas only because, being unmeasurable, they cannot be compared with empirical evidence of existing profitable investment opportunities.

[26]Professor J. J. Spengler has suggested that the reason for this variation lies in the relative strength and size of the "middle class" in different countries at different times. Though undoubtedly a part of the story, it is possible that the middle-class—private enterprise relationship is more a necessary correlation of qualitatively similar categories than an explanation of cause and effect. (cf. Spengler, J. J. "Economic Factors in the Development of Densely Populated Countries." *Proceedings of the American Philosophical Society*, Feb. 1951, p. 22).

methods for attenuating them. There are welcome signs that economists and sociologists are moving in this direction, and in the process are attempting to build a much needed interdisciplinary bridge among the social sciences.[27] It is beyond the scope of this study to elaborate on the work being done, but a few general observations might be made on the general subject of barriers to entrepreneurship in underdeveloped economies, and on the existence of local "islands of entrepreneurship," in many of the underdeveloped countries, which apparently show little tendency toward expansion and diffusion.

Barriers to entrepreneurship may be usefully classified in terms of socio-economic values or propensities, and socio-economic structure. Values represent the society's "more or less unconscious assumptions respecting what is desirable,"[28] and social structure reflects the concrete embodiment of these values in terms of economic and other institutions which are usually designed to assure conformity to social values. Societies whose values are "tradition-directed," as David Riesman has used this term, place a premium on the repetition of an established pattern in economic life, family life, religious life. Institutions in such societies prevent or limit deviations from the established pattern, and hence focus on status and result in stasis. Entrepreneurship and innovation inherently involve a disruption of status and a potential disturbance to social relationships. In such societies, entrepreneurship is thus discouraged by prevailing attitudes and prevented by established institutions, even in the face of demonstrable economic benefits that would result from innovation.

The important relationship between values and institutions is obvious. Professor Gershenkron has suggested that adverse social values or attitudes may not be effective deterrents to the emergence of entrepreneurship, given the existence of adequate incentives, unless these attitudes are "allowed to become crystallized in government action."[29] The proposition might be reformulated to the effect that social values are not likely to be effective deterrents to the emergence of entrepreneurship unless crystallized in adverse institutions. Credit facilities, which involve exorbitant interest charges or excessive collateral requirements, on borrowing for new ventures, are an example of the crystallization of adverse social values into deterrent institu-

---

[27]Among economists, the work of Yale Brozen at Northwestern, Joseph Spengler at Duke, Walt Rostow at M. I. T. and Alexander Gershenkron at Harvard deserve mention. Among sociologists and anthropologists, perhaps the most directly relevant work is being done by Marion Levy at Princeton, and Sol Tax at Chicago.

[28]J. J. Spengler, "Sociological Value Theory, Economic Analyses and Economic Policy," *American Economic Review*, May 1953, p. 342.

[29]Gershenkron, A. "Social Attitudes, Entrepreneurship and Economic Development," *Explorations in Entrepreneurial History*, Oct. 1953, p. 15.

tions. Educational curricula, whose teaching materials, at the lower levels, concentrate on the pattern, myths and purposes of the past, and, at the upper levels, frequently implant the colonially-received cult of the Victorian gentleman, provide another example of the institutional expression of adverse social values.

In private conversation, Chandler Morse of Cornell has suggested a line of inquiry which may be an important qualification to the above discussion. In considering the relationships between socio-economic institutions and entrepreneurship, he suggests that perhaps more significant than the extent to which institutions are "hostile" to entrepreneurship or to economic growth in general, is the extent to which institutions are flexible or rigid to change. "Some societies," he has suggested, "appear to have been exceedingly successful in achieving the right kind of flexibility . . . and hence opening up new opportunities. Others seem to have been inhibited by persistent rigidities. If this is so can we determine why some societies are inherently more flexible than others, and how rigid societies can achieve greater flexibility?" Morse's formulation suggests the desirability of attempting to devise measures of the rigidity of social institutions,[30] and thereby to determine their relative susceptibility to change.

In relating these general considerations more specifically to the underdeveloped countries, one is struck by the fact that a scattering of indigenous entrepreneurship can frequently be found in these countries. The Tatas in India, the Adamjees in Pakistan, the Tans in Malaya and Indonesia are some prominent examples. How these islands of entrepreneurship have come to exist in the midst of adverse socio-economic values and institutions, and why they do not tend to diffuse through the society, become crucial questions if the stimulation of entrepreneurship is as basic to capital formation in the underdeveloped countries as has been suggested.

Professors Boulding at Michigan,[31] Brozen[32] at Northwestern and Handlin at Harvard, have considered this apparent ecological anomaly in terms of "outgroups" which, though living in the local scene, are beyond the restraint of established values and institutions. Such groups (of whom the Parsee Tatas in India are one example, and the Chinese Tans in Southeast Asia another) are able to respond freely to existing investment incentives, and perhaps have a special urge to do so, precisely because they are not integrated into local society. The economic roles of the Jews in many coun-

[30]Professor Gershenkron has expressed the same idea in his notion of "coefficients of changeability" to measure the "degree of persistence in value systems," ibid., p. 13.
[31]Boulding, Kenneth, *Religious Foundations of Economic Progress, Harvard Business Review,* May 1952, p. 36.
[32]Brozen, Yale, "Determinants of Entrepreneurial Ability," *Social Research,* Autumn 1954, pp. 345-49.

tries, the Syrians in Brazil, Argentina and Africa, and the Chinese and Indians in Southeast Asia, all are examples of the same phenomenon.

This approach only partly answers the problem. There are, for example, a few notable cases of indigenous entrepreneurs in South and Southeast Asia who are now, and apparently have always been, fully accepted in the established society. The Adamjees in Pakistan, Mehtas and Birlas in India, and Dasaad Musin, and others in Indonesia are such cases. Specific studies of these and other cases might yield some useful hypotheses concerning the emergence of entrepreneurship.

Of even greater importance, from the standpoint of possible program measures designed to evoke and diffuse indigenous entrepreneurship, is a better understanding of the process by which institutions and societies initially adverse to the emergence of entrepreneurship, become modified to a point where they are receptive to, and even generative of, entrepreneurship. Historical experience suggests that there is a process or processes through which a non-entrepreneurially oriented society fairly quickly changes its orientation, leading to a rapid transmission of the entrepreneurial function throughout society. The Reformation in the 15th century in relation to the Industrial Revolution in the West, and the Meiji Restoration in 19th century Japan, were processes of massive and rapid social change by which tradition-directed institutions and societies were converted into change-directed and entrepreneur-evoking institutions and societies.

Weber and Tawney plausibly represented the Reformation as a process in which an initial religious protest, with strong political support, became the vehicle for an intensification of the secularism and individualism that had already begun to erode medieval civilization in the 14th century Renaissance. Through the intensification of secularism and individualism, the economic growth of the West was activated by the juncture of existing resources and existing investment opportunities under the stimulus of the entrepreneurship unleashed by the Reformation.

As a parallel process, the Meiji Restoration in late 19th century Japan began as a political protest against the weakness and corruption of the Tokugawa shogunate, and issued in a conscious policy of secularism and economic development.[33] Individualism was extraneous to the genesis and motivation behind the Meiji Restoration, whereas individualism was inherent in the genesis of the Reformation. For this reason, especially, the entrepreneurial function was to a considerable extent initially exercised by the state in Japan, only later devolving on individual families as chosen instruments.

---

[33]Allen, C. D. *A Short Economic History of Modern Japan,* London, 1946; and Levy, Marion, "Contrasting Factors in the Modernization of China and Japan," op. cit., p. 190-1.

This oversimplified analysis of Western development has become a generally accepted part of economic history. Perhaps because of its general acceptance, the analysis has not been pushed much beyond the stage at which Weber and Tawney left it. Specifically, a variety of questions involving the genesis of entrepreneurship, the reasons for its appearance at variable rates in different places and among different groups, the reasons for the transition from the entrepreneurship of the merchant to that of the producer, and many others, have not been raised, let alone answered.[84] Recently, interest in this subject in relation to the problems of underdeveloped areas has been reawakened, and its potential importance from the standpoint of program requirements, recognized. Simon Kuznets,[85] in particular, noting that the breadth of international disparities in per capita real income between the "developed" and "underdeveloped" countries is a relatively recent phenomenon, has strongly urged a reexamination of historical material with a view to shedding greater light on the nature (and policy implications) of the transition from tradition-directed to technology-and-production-directed values and institutions in the West and Japan.

Perhaps the most fundamental implication of the previous discussion from the standpoint of evoking entrepreneurship in Asia and the Near East today is that, on the broad level of socio-economic values and institutions, the diffusion and expansion of entrepreneurship requires a social change of the scope and intensity of the Reformation in the West and the Meiji Restoration in Japan.

In societies lacking an entrepreneurial orientation or élite, Communism offers itself as a vehicle for accomplishing the ends that elsewhere have been accomplished by enterprise—namely a higher income and a better life. This is a great strength in its appeal. At the same time, its great weakness lies in the fact that, unlike the historical analogies previously cited, it is *externally* conceived, originated, and directed. Both from the political standpoint of a counter appeal to communism, and the socio-economic

---

[84]The work of the Harvard Research Center in Entrepreneurial History, though resulting in many important publications, has not really tried to deal with many of the questions in entrepreneurial history most relevant to the problems of underdeveloped countries today. But many works of the Center deserve mention as furnishing especially useful raw materials for further analysis, for example, *Change and the Entrepreneur*, Cambridge 1949; the six volumes of the Journal published by the Center entitled *Explorations in Entrepreneurial History;* Landes, D. S., *"French Entrepreneurship and Industrial Growth in the Nineteenth Century"* Journal of Economic History, May 1949; and many other works.

[85]See Kuznets, S. "International Differences in Income Levels: Some Reflections on Their Causes." *Economic Development and Cultural Change*, April 1953, pp. 19, 25-6.

standpoint of effectively evoking indigenous entrepreneurship, a basic question is whether there is any movement *already* established and operative in the Near East and Asian areas which has the kinetic or potential social energy capable of effecting the fundamental social changes historically brought about by the Reformation in the West and the Imperial Restoration in Japan?

As a tentative hypothesis it might be suggested that the dynamism frequently associated with nationalism in these areas may be capable of effecting the changes in attitudes, career preferences and institutions on which the diffusion and expansion of entrepreneurship depend. The usefulness of the hypothesis clearly depends on whether or not methods and programs can be devised for transmuting the drive and energy of the post-World War II nationalist movements in this region into channels of innovation, enterprise and production. Plainly this task involves an effort in *conscious* "social engineering" which is vast and of unclear dimensions. There is also the question of the time required for the economic consequence of the Reformation, and even of the more intensified Restoration in Japan, to materialize. Yet it may be suggested that just as the latecomers to economic development are able to telescope many technological changes which in their origin required slow and laborious progress, so they may be able to telescope and accelerate the social changes which historically have stimulated entrepreneurship and economic growth.

The many problems suggested by this approach cannot be fully enumerated here. For example, the objection might be raised that in origin and motivation, the nationalist movements in this region have primarily been negative forces directed *against* established foreign control, and hence their capacity to serve the positive purposes of stimulating entrepreneurship may be doubtful. Moreover, to the extent that the negative force of nationalism has been associated with the advocacy of specific programs, especially in South and Southeast Asia, it has frequently been antagonistic to private entrepreneurship.

Neither of these objections is conclusive. As already noted, both the Reformation and the Meiji Restoration were initially negative protests whose positive consequences for the emergence of indigenous enterprise came *after* the "negative" objectives (e.g. hierarchic separation from Rome, expulsion of the Shogunate) had been achieved. The antagonism of Asian nationalism to private entrepreneurship is not clearly structured. It has stemmed in part, from the assumed link between private entrepreneurship and foreign political control. To this extent it may have been reduced by the achievement of political independence in much of this region. To a considerable extent the opposition of even Asian "socialists" to private entrepreneurship is functional rather than ideological. They have

tended to look exclusively to public entrepreneurship to undertake investment because of the lack of indigenous private sources of initiative and
innovation. If methods can be devised for channeling the emotional ener-
gies of nationalism into the stimulation of indigenous enterprise, then indeed it may be found that the highly nationalistic "socialists" of the region
may not only support, but become the leaders in, indigenous entrepreneurial activity.

To relate the foregoing more directly to problems of capital formation,
the approach we have suggested might be summed up as follows: If increased capital formation in this region depends significantly on evoking
indigenous entrepreneurship, and if the broad problem of evoking entrepreneurship partly involves devising or utilizing a suitable engine of social
change, the still unexpended force of nationalism in Asia and the Near
East may be capable of providing the required dynamism. Measures, in the
area of what Professor Spengler has called "manipulative economics," to
harness and direct this dynamism, then become a directly relevant part of
the problem of capital formation.

The approach suggested is implicit in some of the operating techniques
now being used in this region. The community development program in
India, for example, has consciously tried to affect attitudes toward technological change, by extension methods which try to relate the adoption of
improved practices to patriotism and national pride.

Moreover, in many cases, the problem of evoking entrepreneurship may
in fact be simpler than would appear from the previous discussion. To
some extent the required changes in values and attitudes may have already
occurred in some of the underdeveloped countries. That the change remains ineffective may be due to the durability of institutions adverse to
entrepreneurship, rather than to established values and attitudes, which
are, in fact, already undergoing sharp changes. The experience of the Sears
Roebuck Company in Mexico, where it was able to find and develop, in
the space of five years, 1300 small local suppliers producing 80 per cent of
its gross annual retail volume of Mexico, suggests that (1) there may be a
greater entrepreneurial potential in some of the underdeveloped economies than we would at first suspect, and (2) appropriate institutional
innovations and program measures can rapidly translate this potential into
sharply accelerated investment and output.[36]

[36]See Richardson Wood and Virginia Keyser, "The Case Study of Sears Roebuck de Mexico, S. A.," National Planning Association, Washington, D. C., May, 1953.

Program Possibilities and Research Needs. This section attempts to translate broader questions of approach and concept into more specific programs of action and research. The link between the specific proposals and the preceding analysis derives from the contribution which the proposals can make to stimulating entrepreneurship and thereby generating an effective demand for productive capital.

In the following summary listing, program possibilities are presented first, though in some cases it will be noted that a program suggestion implies concomitant "study" of the situation to be acted upon and hence the line between research and program is not always clear.

PROGRAM POSSIBILITIES

Notwithstanding the shortage of entrepreneurs and the ineffective demand for capital in general, it has already been noted that in most underdeveloped countries some few indigenous "islands of entrepreneurship" exist. Somehow these anomalies have evolved even though they frequently show little tendency to diffuse. In addition to the more obvious examples of a few large industrial and commercial enterprises, the occasional modern farm, bicycle shop, brick-kilned potter's shop, small brick factory and the like, which are infrequently but invariably encountered some place in each country of this region, exemplify departures from established patterns. Program attention in the underdeveloped countries (and preferably by nationals of the countries), under the sponsorship of private or public foreign or local agencies, should be directed to detailed studies of selected cases of this kind, carefully chosen in terms of size, the indigenous character and the reproducibility of the enterprise concerned. Material covered in the studies, to make them useful, should include financial, cost, market, management, technical and other factors affecting the origin and success of the enterprise.

Not only would such case studies provide useful research material for analyzing whether in fact a reproducible pattern exists for the stimulation of such entrepreneurial islands; in addition, and perhaps more important, such cases would be highly useful, if appropriately documented and illustrated, for the different audiences to which addressed: (1) in method demonstration in community development work; (2) as teaching materials in secondary schools and colleges; and (3) for more general public distribution. Use of such teaching materials might serve a particularly needed function in institutions of higher education in attracting attention of intellectuals to the challenge, opportunities and emoluments of entrepreneurship.

Entrepreneurship need not be exercised only by individuals or by the state. The range of possible forms which the function can take is much wider. Western corporate and cooperative experience itself suggests that various kinds of group organizations can exercise entrepreneurial responsibility. In many of the underdeveloped countries of the Asian and Near Eastern area, the possibility of devising forms of "community entrepreneurship" may be particularly promising. Such forms accord more closely with indigenous *mores* which frequently countenance and encourage action by the group rather than the individual, or at least more readily accept individual action when it embraces participation by the group. At the same time, the role of community entrepreneurship in increasing and mobilizing local savings, and in applying the possibilities of efficient, labor-intensive techniques to local industry may be highly important.

One method for achieving these multiple objectives may lie in the use of an adapted form of community lotteries as a means of stimulating community entrepreneurship.[87] National lotteries have, of course, been frequently used in Puerto Rico, Mexico and other South American countries as a means of mobilizing savings for general investment purposes. This technique could be adapted in several ways to help in stimulating local entrepreneurship, as well as mobilizing and increasing local savings for investment purposes:

(a) the lottery could be placed on a community rather than national basis, organized perhaps through the local extension or community development service; (b) net proceeds could be exclusively used for investment within the community; and (c) losing tickets could represent, or be convertible into, equity shares in the investment undertaken with the net proceeds of the lottery, and as such would constitute a stake in the ownership and a claim on the earnings of the enterprise. For example, investment of the net proceeds of a lottery in a brick kiln, locally-powered metal working shop, or small cement plant, in the community would presumably yield net earnings in the future. The earnings would then accrue to the "community entrepreneurs" through stock dividends; (d) local unskilled labor costs frequently comprise 40-60 per cent of the capital required for construction and other expenses connected with establishing local enterprises. An effort could be made through the lottery to mobilize underemployed labor for meeting these expenses, thereby freeing the net proceeds of the lottery for equipment or materials costs to the ultimate benefit of the community entrepreneurs. This could be done by making the convertibility of lottery tickets into equity shares contingent on the validated contribution of a stipulated amount of labor services, as portage or construction.

Clearly, the bulk of the effort and financing involved in this program would be contributed by the community. However, external assistance could set the process in motion on an initial pilot-project basis, and per-

[87]Professor Sufrin has expressed reservations concerning this approach.

form a continuing service by developing and "packaging" a range of capital facilities—in terms of sizes, costs and designs of different kinds of plant. The potential community entrepreneurs could then choose from this range, in deciding what productive facility they wished to create.

Through methods of this type lotteries could be developed to utilize existing social habits while converting their essence from chance and consumption to chance and investment.

A brief reference has already been made to the method used by one American retailer in Mexico in stimulating local entrepreneurship. Essentially, this method involved the creation of a centralized, urban distribution facility for marketing a variety of commodities whose production was contracted-out to many small, semi-rural shops in the vicinity. The required local entrepreneurship was built up by locating existing handicraft shops nearby, providing and demonstrating a particular product design, and then frequently advancing needed machinery or working capital against scheduled delivery of finished or semi-finished items. The range and volume of supplies handled in this way in Mexico, and the phenomenal growth which has attended the operations of some of the local entrepreneurs in the process,[38] would not have to be equalled to make a program along these lines worth stimulating in other countries.

As a first step, market surveys should be made in one or two of the underdeveloped countries in the Asian and Near East region to determine the range of commodities presently marketable in selected urban areas and capable of small-scale local fabrication. The market surveys could draw especially on import lists and on items already produced domestically which are now in insufficient supply or are expected to be in increasing demand in the near future. Notwithstanding the market limitations already noted in underdeveloped countries, it might be expected that such surveys would encompass quite a wide variety of products.

It should be emphasized that the reference to the Sears Roebuck experience in Mexico does not imply that foreign capital is required for this kind of enterprise. With the findings of market surveys available, it may be possible to bring these opportunities to the attention of local financial interests and thereby induce the creation of a central marketing facility. The central marketing mechanism would then serve as an important bridge between the urban market and the rural producer or potential producer. As a second step, an additional inducement might be offered in the form of providing some small amounts of credit for machinery and materials as an advance to local suppliers, along the lines followed by Sears Roebuck in Mexico.

[38]See Wood, R., op. cit., pp. 39-45.

It has already been noted that adverse socio-economic institutions can hinder the emergence of entrepreneurship despite the existence of strong economic incentives and despite the modification of socio-economic values that may already have occurred. Credit institutions are frequently among the most difficult obstacles confronting potential entrepreneurs.[89] Frequently in the Asian and Near Eastern countries new productive ventures are prevented or restricted by particular credit practices. The charging of excessive and frequently prohibitive interest rates is widespread and well known. Perhaps less well known is the frequent practice of requiring collateral of such magnitude that this, rather than the interest rate, is the effective deterrent to new capital ventures. In the Philippines, for example, new loans in urban areas frequently carry an interest charge of only 8 per cent while the collateral requirement may be 200 to 300 per cent of the loan. At the same time, loans for agricultural improvement in rural areas, where collateral is limited, frequently carry interest charges up to 150 per cent per annum.

To test the extent to which such practices may be impeding the emergence of entrepreneurship, a program along the following lines might be instituted, with foreign private or public assistance as appropriate, on a pilot demonstration basis in one or more localized areas in the Asian and Near Eastern region: 1) a guarantee fund could be created in favor of an indigenous public agency through administrative arrangements suitable to the particular country situation. The agency might then agree with an established financial institution or institutions that on new loans for productive purposes up to 75 per cent of the usual collateral requirement would be borne by the fund at a zero or nominal interest charge, thereby relieving the potential borrower of this requirement; 2) through a local community development or extension service in rural areas not served by established banking institutions, a public loan fund could be set up in a pilot area. The loan fund would be available for productive loans at an interest charge of say 50 per cent of prevailing commercial rates.

The purpose of both of these devices would be to test the extent to which the shortage of entrepreneurship is caused by unfavorable credit institutions and practices.

The schools of business administration in the United States may have some particular contribution to make to developing methods for evoking entrepreneurship in underdeveloped areas. As Professor Schumpeter has observed, there is frequently only a fine line between the function of entre-

---

[89]It might be mentioned that this reference is to the institutional aspects of credit. In terms of the previous discussion of existing and potential savings, the shortage of credit may, in many of the underdeveloped countries, be regarded as more fundamentally due to an inadequacy in practices than to a shortage of resources.

preneurship and "creative" business management or administration.[40] By virtue of their considerable attention to the phenomenon of entrepreneurship in American business history, the business schools may have accumulated a body of experience that would be highly useful in meeting this problem in the underdeveloped areas.

This experience might be drawn upon in at least two ways. At the broad policy level, a meeting of representatives of the major business schools could be convened to establish a consensus as to whether and how these institutions can assist in evoking entrepreneurial inclination and talents in the underdeveloped countries. The purpose of such a meeting would be to consider such questions as: whether or not entrepreneurs can be trained; the similarities and dissimilarities in curricula for management executives and entrepreneurs; the relevance of U. S. entrepreneurial experience, and its possible reproducibility in the underdeveloped countries; the nature of the transition from the entrepreneurship of the merchant to that of the producer. The consensus of the group on such questions as these would provide a basis for future policy and research activity.

At a more specific level, it would be desirable for one or more schools of business administration to undertake curriculum development in the field of comparative entrepreneurial history. This undertaking would involve analysis of historical experience in different countries with respect to the occurrence, extension, forms and patterns of entrepreneurship. As an adjunct to this effort, a text containing readings in entrepreneurial case materials might be compiled, consisting of material from Western, Japanese, and other experience, selected for its applicability to the problem of entrepreneurship in the underdeveloped countries and for its bearing on the kinds of questions mentioned above. Such a text would have usefulness not only in training which American schools might offer students from the underdeveloped countries, but also in the curricula taught in institutions in these countries themselves.

RESEARCH NEEDS

On the broader level of analyzing economic history and comparative socio-economic institutions, a closer study is needed of the precise relationship between the Reformation and the Meiji Restoration as causes or influences, and the emergence of entrepreneurship as consequence, in the West and Japan, respectively. Is, first of all, the basic thesis that implies the existence of such a relationship valid, and how can it be tested? What was the organic pattern of cause and consequence in these two instances of broad social change? What is there that is reproducible in this pattern?

[40]Schumpeter, in *Change and the Entrepreneur*, op. cit., p. 68.

Moving beyond the specific thesis itself, a variety of other questions relating to the historical rise of entrepreneurship is suggested by our previous analysis. What, for example, were the effects of the early manifestations of both public and private entrepreneurship on the volume and pattern of capital formation in the West and Japan? Were the historical excesses and abuses of entrepreneurship necessary to the achievement of the rates and kinds of capital formation attained? Can coefficients, or at least criteria, of flexibility or changeability of different societies be devised to measure the receptivity of these societies to those kinds of institutional changes or innovations which are likely to promote entrepreneurship and economic development more generally? What role was played by entrepreneurial "outgroups" in different countries and at different periods, in terms of their disproportionate influence on the volume and pattern of capital formation? Is there any identifiable and reproducible pattern by which the entrepreneurship of an outgroup becomes more widely diffused throughout society?

These are some of the questions that need to be emphasized and do not appear to be receiving adequate consideration by research presently underway. To a considerable extent, this needed research calls for an analytical review of economic history from the *standpoint of the problems and programs of the underdeveloped countries today*. Economic history is not usually approached in operational or program terms although historical analogies may be able to provide helpful insights into the problems of underdeveloped countries today. The reconsideration of economic history from the standpoint of hypotheses and questions suggested by current problems of development should be of considerable value.

Besides the broader questions involving a reconsideration and reinterpretation of economic history, empirical research is needed to test the validity of two main hypotheses advanced in the preceding analysis.

The first hypothesis suggested that aggregate resource shortages were frequently not the major deterrent to the increased formation of productive capital. Several kinds of empirical research are needed to test this hypothesis. This research requires more detailed studies in several of the countries of the Near East and South and Southeast Asia, of (a) the volume and pattern of *current* savings and investment; (b) the volume and character of accumulated "passive" capital and its susceptibility to mobilization for productive investment; (c) the pattern of consumption, especially in rural areas and the estimated marginal propensity to consume (and save) as deducible from changes over time in income and consumption; (d) whether, in underdeveloped countries, the savings and investment functions tend to be determined by the same variables—a point that was alluded to in connection with the discussion of "non-transferable" rural savings—as in developed countries; and (e) whether the marginal propensity to consume of upper income groups tends to be higher and that of lower income groups lower than might be inferred from Western experience.

These are all basic research requirements for further work on capital formation. To a surprising extent, theorizing on the subject is frequently received opinion based on conjecture concerning these questions of fact.

The second hypothesis contended that many profitable investment opportunities typically exist in these countries given the present market situation and even given the present level of technological knowledge. Empirically, this hypothesis might be tested by an investigation in one or more underdeveloped countries of small-scale, productive and profitable investment opportunities, requiring only small amounts of capital and, frequently, techniques which are already known in the country concerned. Such an investigation would provide and analyze the relevant cost and market data on selected internal investment opportunities, and attempt to learn whether there is any geographic or social pattern in the occurrence of this range of unexploited opportunities.

One of the vexing problems in discussions of underdeveloped countries is the very name! No nation enjoys the designation "underdeveloped." Nor does the word generally signify in this context anything but a poor country or one living below its reasonable potential. There now exists no general agreement as to the characteristics or attributes of underdeveloped-ness. One of the authors therefore suggested a comparative socio-economic analysis of underdeveloped countries, if for no other purpose than to define the universe of discourse. In reality the results even of purely taxonomic study would probably be more useful than mere definition, which would be invaluable in itself. It is suggested that significant and relevant social, resource, economic, political, and cultural factors be classified into some system of ordinal measures, and related to specific countries, regions, and sub-regions.[41]

[41]Compare the reference in Chapter Six to the propositional inventory relating to economic development and cultural change which is being undertaken by the University of Chicago. Infra, p. 114.

CHAPTER THREE

TECHNOLOGICAL ALTERNATIVES AND THE OPTIMUM USE OF CAPITAL

The Problem. The previous discussion has concentrated on the proposition that both resources and productive opportunities presently exist in the underdeveloped countries of Asia and the Near East for substantially increasing capital formation. The analysis, as well as recommendations for action in both program and research terms, therefore centered on the problem of increasing the demand for capital by evoking indigenous entrepreneurship in order that existing resources and investment opportunities may together yield an accelerated rate of investment.

Of parallel importance to increasing the rate and thereby the quantity of capital formation, is to achieve maximum productivity from any given amount of capital. As already suggested, pattern and quality of investment are both of importance in the process of economic development. How, then, can a newly developing country secure the optimum investment pattern, in the sense of achieving maximum productivity from a growing capital stock, over a specified period of time? Can criteria be formulated for guiding investment decisions, and can techniques be used to determine the optimum investment of any given amount of capital for any particular sector of the economy, as well as for the economy as a whole? Do some sectors play an initiating, and other an adaptive, role in the process of development, and, if so, how can these various roles be foreseen and applied to the determination of investment decisions?

These questions involve complex theoretical and practical issues concerning economic structure and processes. A summary of research in this vitally important field of investment criteria indicates three major developments of interest to the problems considered in this study:

(a) Technological change and technological alternatives,

(b) Techniques for determining optimum investment; and

(c) The idea of "leading growth" sectors.

TECHNOLOGICAL CHANGE AND TECHNOLOGICAL ALTERNATIVES

Abstracting from a special definition used in static economic theory, the term technological change is generally used to describe any change in production techniques whether or not previously known. In terms of guiding new investment decisions, technological change is significant because it raises productivity, i.e., it enables either greater output to take place with given capital and other resources (or with increased resources which are small relative to the increased output), or the continuation of a given output with a smaller use of resources.

The quantitative role of technological change in economic development is substantial. For example, it has been estimated that of the fourfold increment in the United States gross national product during the first half of the 20th century, one-half is due to increased capital and labor, and the remaining half is attributable to technological change. Capital formation is usually closely associated with technological change whenever rapid growth in real per capita output occurs, although Kuznets has noted certain apparent inconsistencies in the relationship.[42]

The close association between capital formation and technological change has sometimes been overlooked in discussions of economic growth, though much separate attention has been devoted to each of these variables. As a consequence, different individuals and different disciplines have generally worked on the two related subjects. While economists have made aggregative calculations of necessary rates of investment in various growth models, according to assumed capital-output ratios, engineers have made decisions as to the techniques to be used—and the capital required—in different productive projects. The function of capital formation as an essential vehicle for technological change, and the role of technological change as a guide to programming investment, are often inadequately stressed.

To some extent, the separation in economic analysis—until fairly recently—of capital formation and technological change, has been due to the fact that the economist has taken technology as "given" in the construction of growth models and the consideration of growth problems. Typically, in traditional economic writing, technology, or the "state of the arts," has been conceived of as externally determined and hence beyond the frame of reference of the writer. For this reason, much traditional economic writing is scarcely relevant to many of the problems of investment decision-making which confront the underdeveloped countries.

In a sense, programs of foreign technical assistance to underdeveloped areas have also frequently operated on the assumption that technology is a "given." In these cases, it has been assumed that the techniques used in the

---

[42] Kuznets, S. in *Survey of Contemporary Economics*, Vol. II, op. cit., p. 179.

donor country are necessarily appropriate for the recipient country, notwithstanding its different economic structure, resource endowment, social structure, etc. Viewed in this light, technological considerations have generally tended to enter the programming picture *after* the basic investment decision has been made, rather than as a fundamental part of the consideration of alternative investment possibilities.

More recently, economists have been calling increasing attention to the relevance of technological change and technological variability to problems of theory in general and programming in particular. At the level of *weltanschauung*, rather than analysis, Clarence Ayres of Texas University has re-emphasized the need for economists to give increased emphasis to the role of technological change in motivating and reflecting economic growth.[43] Everett Hagen at M.I.T. has stressed the importance of the "habit of technological advance," in motivating capital formation.[44] Wassily Leontief at Harvard has pioneered in developing methods for translating conjecture about technological factors into quantitative measures of the resource requirements associated with a given economic structure. These methods enable, first of all, the calculation of the inter-industry impact of any programmed change in output. Then, by the use of technical coefficients of production, which show the capital and labor requirements per unit of additional output based on the current technological practices of the industries concerned, the Leontief method permits the calculation of the kinds and quantities of capital formation required to achieve the programmed change in output. These methods have generally been applied to analysis and programming in developed countries. Their application and adaptation to the problems of investment programming in underdeveloped countries remains to be done.

At least two other names might be mentioned as particularly prominent in this field of research. On the broad theoretical level, Yale Brozen of the Technological Institute of Northwestern University, has stressed the importance of incorporating technological change in economic theory by an analysis of the "endogenous" determinants of such change. More directly relevant to the programming problems of underdeveloped countries is Brozen's emphasis on the range of technological alternatives open to newly developing countries and his illustration in simplified linear models of the importance of these alternatives in determining investment decisions.[45]

[43]See Ayres, C. "The Role of Technology in Economic Theory," *American Economic Review*—Papers and Proceedings, May 1953, pp. 278-87.
[44]Hagen's formulation recalls our previous discussion of entrepreneurship. Essentially, the entrepreneur is the agent of technological advance. As such, his efforts both reflect and engender the "habit of technological advance" throughout the society.
[45]Yale Brozen, "Determinants of the Direction of Technological Change," *American Economic Review*, May 1953, pp. 293-294 ff.

Henry Aubrey has especially focussed attention on the specific technological features of small industry, as suggested by the mechanical, management and marketing practices of small industry in Japan. At the same time, he has noted an important connection between the use of small-industry technology on the one hand, and, on the other hand, an increased supply of local savings, a more effective utilization of local savings, a more effective utilization of local labor, and a minimum dislocation of the established rural social structure of many of the underdeveloped countries.[46]

The emphasis on technological or process variability which recurs frequently in current economic writing has direct relevance to a determination of the most productive kinds of capital formation in underdeveloped countries. The most obvious and yet frequently overlooked implication of technological or process variability for developing countries is that the optimum technique for producing a given commodity in a developed economy may not be the optimum technique for producing the same commodity in an underdeveloped economy. The substitutability of factors of production in accord with their relative prices is standard doctrine in economic analysis. What has not always been recognized is the fact that for any given process or technique of production, the substitutability of the factors, e.g. of labor for capital, is not unlimited. Hence, to provide a greater opportunity for factor substitutability, "comparative" or alternative technologies must be studied, with particular reference to the physical and social resources which are available in the underdeveloped countries.

Western industrial technology has typically involved the organization of large-scale production units, with heavy concentrations of capital located in urban areas close to markets. In underdeveloped countries, there are many reasons for questioning the applicability of this technology as a general rule. The different relative prices of the factors of production in the underdeveloped areas has already been alluded to.[47] In addition, the use of

[46]Aubrey, "The Role of Small Industry," op. cit., p. 295 ff.
[47]Professor A. E. Kahn at Cornell has contested the thesis that the scarcity of capital in underdeveloped areas suggests that it be used in labor-intensive and capital-saving ways. His view is that a capital-saving technique (i.e., one in which the ratio of capital to value added is low) may, in fact, involve uneconomic investment. The "correct criterion" to guide investment decision, he argues, is "Social Marginal Productivity," i.e. the *net* contribution of an increment in investment to the national output after full allowance is made for the cost of the labor and materials entering into the value of final output. See Kahn, A. E. "Investment Criteria in Development Programs," *Quarterly Journal of Economics*, February 1951, p. 39. It might be suggested that an investment whose capital-output ratio is low is likely to yield a high social marginal product. The reason for this probability is that in underdeveloped economies, the opportunity cost of labor is frequently nil even though minimum wage laws may disguise this fact. Hence, from the standpoint of social marginal product, much, if not all, of the total output derived from an investment which is labor-using is attributable to the increment in investment. See also H. H. Chenery, "The Application of Investment Criteria," *Quarterly Journal of Economics*, Feb. 1953.

an "urbanized" technology, involving large concentrations of capital, creates a need in the underdeveloped economies for large amounts of overhead social capital in the form of housing and sanitation facilities. Part of the need for overhead capital facilities can perhaps be avoided if, for example, technology is adopted which permits decentralization of production.[48]

Does this line of thinking imply that the underdeveloped countries should retrace the technological evolution of the West if they wish to maximize the return from new capital formation? The answer to this question is not simple. There may be cases where investment identified with a technology which the West has "outgrown" would be advisable on grounds of maximizing productivity and minimizing costs. Small forges for making steel plow points are a case in point. There are no doubt other cases where investment in a facility technologically identified with a current process in the West is warranted. The production of fertilizer on a scale, and using the techniques, current in the West may be a case in point. Here the exceedingly limited range of technological alternatives available, and the high productivity of the advanced technique, more than outweighs the different resource pattern, factor price parities, and socio-economic structure characterizing the underdeveloped economy.

Finally, there may be still other cases in which the technology most appropriate to a particular investment decision in the underdeveloped countries will be one neither presently nor previously in operation. From any array of technological alternatives open to a newly developing country, the question of choice may be simpler and less important than the need for further adaptation to suit the socio-economic circumstances of the country concerned. Given a wide array of technological alternatives, the scope for developing new technological innovations, by modification and combination of various alternatives, is considerably broader than was the case when the original technological changes were developed.[49]

On the inductive level, it may well be that current Japanese processes and techniques have more relevance to investment needs and possibilities

[48]The frequent assumption that decentralization of industrial location would involve countervailing overhead costs for transportation is only valid if it is assumed that local producing units must service or be serviced from distant markets, a point which would seem to be contradicted by the existence of opportunities for competitive small scale fabrication of a variety of commodities. See Aubrey, H. op. cit., p. 300.

[49]Dr. Kuznets has emphasized the importance of technological variability in economic development by this novel formulation of the historical problem of poverty in the underdeveloped countries: "The have-not societies are poor because they have not succeeded in overcoming scarcity of natural resources by appropriate changes in technology, not because the scarcity of resources is an inexorable factor for which there is no remedy." "International Income Differences: Reflections on Their Causes," in *Economic Development and Cultural Change*, April 1953, p. 12.

in the underdeveloped countries than the current technology of the West.[50] Although considerably more study of this point is needed before it can be established, the conclusion might nevertheless be inferred from the fact that the socio-economic environment, in which Japanese technology evolved, was in many respects more nearly similar to the present environment of the underdeveloped areas in Asia and the Near East than was the environment in which Western technology evolved. It may even be suggested that present industrial technology in the West might have turned out quite differently if the range of technological choices which subsequently became available had been known at the time the Western economies were becoming structured. Henry Aubrey has well expressed this idea:

> The Industrial Revolution was based on the use of steam as motive power and remained dependent on this source of energy for over a century. Large size and concentration of operations . . . resulted. This type of organization was well established by the time the generation of power on a small scale by the internal combustion engine and the decentralized use of power through the electric motor became economical. It would be idle to speculate on what effect the availability of this equipment early in the course of Western industrialization might have had on the size of plants . . . and the concentration of industry. . . . Such speculation, however, is not only justifiable but highly desirable in considering the future locations and size-cost relationship in the developing countries. . . . Since these considerations raise strong doubts whether currently developing countries must fully repeat the pattern we associate with Western industrialization, the task of outlining the other, and possibly more appropriate, patterns is legitimate.[51]

If an efficient, decentralized locational pattern, consisting of modern but smaller-scale producing units, can be devised for industrial organization in the underdeveloped countries, the effect in reducing overhead capital requirements may be quite substantial. In consequence a greater proportion of capital formation in developing countries might be channeled toward those investments which have a relatively low ratio of fixed capital to output, and hence have a significant and rapid effect on the use of idle resources and the rate of growth.[52]

---

[50]See for some suggestive material on Japanese technology and industrial organization, Uyeda, T. *The Small Industries of Japan,* New York, 1938.

[51]Aubrey, op. cit., p. 270.

[52]It should also be noted that the development of atomic power may provide energy in any area within a given country at nearly constant cost, because the cost of transporting fuel would be negligible by comparison with the present costs of transporting coal or transmitting power by grid. This potential narrowing of regional differences in power costs may have highly significant implications for a more dispersed location of new industry in developing countries. See Schurr, S., and Marschak, J., *Economic Aspects of Atomic Power,* Princeton, 1950, p. 4.

To sum up: insufficient research and program attention have been devoted to technological variability as an aid to guiding capital formation in the underdeveloped areas into fields of maximum productivity. On the research side, this lack has perhaps been related to the economist's frequent assumption that technological change is an "exogenous" variable and should be assumed rather than analyzed.

If the research lack has been due to the assumptions of the economist, on the program side the lack of attention to technological variability has perhaps been due to the behavioral patterns of engineers! It is questionable whether, in approaching the blueprinting of industrial or utilities projects in the underdeveloped areas, Western-trained supervisory engineers, have thought in terms of a full range of technological alternatives which could be evaluated in terms of relative factor prices and indigenous social structure before arriving at a decision as to the optimum method to be used. Dams can be built with hand labor or bulldozers; factories can be vertically-integrated fabricating plants or assembly units for work that is subcontracted in small shops; cement plants can be (competitively) scaled to a weekly output of four hundred bags or a thousand times this amount; sulfuric acid plants can be competitive at an output of four tons per week under certain circumstances or a much larger amount under others.[53] It may well be that the engineers, who usually make the major operating decisions in development projects, actually and operationally regard the production function as a single process line with only scale variability. The American engineer is familiar with and trained in the current technology of the United States; he is, generally, not familiar either with previous technological practice in the United States or with current practice in other countries. If he is called upon to blueprint an industrial or construction project, his advice must generally reflect what he is familiar with.

An implication of the foregoing is that a series of quantitative analyses should be made of the technological alternatives that actually exist in the construction, equipping and operation of a variety of plants and projects in both the capital and consumer goods fields. Kenneth Bohr of the International Bank has suggested the classification of technological variability in manufacturing industry in terms of four measurable criteria: (1) capital-output ratios; (2) concentrated vs. decentralized location; (3) scale of plant; and (4) skilled vs. unskilled labor requirements.[54] Bohr has developed quantitative indexes for each of these criteria, and has made some preliminary measurements for comparable industries in the United States,

---

[53]Aubrey, op. cit., p. 300.
[54]See Bohr, K., *"Investment Criteria for Manufacturing Industries,"* The *Review of Economics and Statistics,* May 1954.

United Kingdom and Australia. The extent of variation uncovered by his estimates, even in countries which one might have thought use similar technology, is quite significant. The result suggests that a substantial extension and elaboration of this empirical approach—in time as well as in space—would be particularly useful in uncovering a full range or inventory of both international and inter-temporal technological alternatives from which newly developing countries might choose on the basis of their resources, social endowments and program objectives. Japanese technology might fruitfully be analyzed from this standpoint.[55]

TECHNIQUES FOR DETERMINING OPTIMUM INVESTMENT[56]

Reference has already been made to the technique of structural, inter-industry analysis developed by Professor Leontief and its probable, but untested, relevance for investment decision-making in underdeveloped countries. For present purposes, the Leontief method might be summarized in three analytical steps: (1) an analysis of the transactions between each "industry" or sector in a particular national or regional economic unit and all of the other industries or sectors, including the "outside world" as a separate sector. This aggregative compilation shows the total flow of goods and services in the economy, including exports and imports. It enables a calculation of the extent to which each sector must increase its output in order to achieve a programmed increase in final demand for the goods or services of any particular sector or of the economy as a whole; (2) independently of the inter-sectoral calculations, an analysis *within each sector* of the capital that must be on hand for the operation of the sector con-

---

[55]It should be emphasized that the analysis here suggested involves ramified problems of defining and identifying comparable "industries" or projects in different countries, and of collecting comparable data on the kinds and amounts of labor and capital and the location and scale of operations. Moreover, the four categories for measuring technological variability which Bohr has used are not the only relevant ones. The wide variations in labor-management relations and practices in different countries, and even within countries, and the major effect which such variations have on productivity, suggest that this is another category in which variability measurement would be highly useful for investment decision-making in underdeveloped areas.

[56]In large part, the discussion of techniques, as well as the preceding discussion of technological alternatives, suggests a context of programming and decision-making by public authorities. This may seem inconsistent when viewed in the light of the previous emphasis on private entrepreneurship. Two comments might be made on this possible criticism. First, entrepreneurship will, in the Asian and Near East region, at least to some extent be exercised through public channels and institutions. This being the case, it is important that the investment decisions made by public agencies be directly related to explicitly formulated "optimization" principles. Secondly, techniques for reaching optimum investment decisions can also assist entrepreneurship in two ways: by directly helping private industry to reach optimum investment decisions as is presently beginning to be done in the U. S., and by stimulating private entrepreneurship generally in response to better public investment decisions.

cerned at a particular level of output. These "stock" requirements can be expressed as technical coefficients of production showing the ratio of capital[57] required per unit of current operating capacity for the sector concerned; (3) by a combination of the inter-sectoral impact of a given program objective calculated in (1), and the technical (stock) coefficients of production calculated in (2), the particular amounts and kinds of capital formation needed to achieve the program objectives can be computed.

This technique has been usefully applied to a variety of defense programming problems in the United States.

Though there are certain obvious parallels between the procedure described above and the problem of investment programming in underdeveloped countries, there are important respects in which this technique is not fully applicable to the development context. The input-output technique generally takes the present economic structure and the technology it reflects as given. The technical coefficients of production as well as the inter-sectoral flows measured by the Leontief methods are normally those which reflect and comprise the *present* structure of the economy. From the standpoint of a highly developed economy, like that of the United States, this frame of reference is often reasonable for forward planning purposes. Here the problem is achieving an optimum allocation of resources for stipulated program aims with a given technology and economic structure.

In the underdeveloped areas, on the contrary, the problem is rather one of achieving an optimum allocation of resources by *changing the technology and structure of the economy*. In one case, technology and structure are already the result of a long series of changes; hence, they are not likely to change substantially again *within the planning period*. In the underdeveloped areas, by contrast, present technology and structure are often largely unchanged from what they were several hundred years ago. Change in technology and economic structure is the essence of the development problem within the planning period. Hence, investment programming must consciously take into account the technological and structural alternatives open to it in achieving stipulated objectives.

One obvious implication is that the input-output technique, to be usefully adapted to problems of investment programming in underdeveloped areas, must incorporate an array of technological alternatives or variable technical coefficients, of the kind suggested above.[58] The achievement of an optimum pattern of investment must be considered in terms of a choice among these technological alternatives.

---

[57]Separate coefficients for different kinds of capital (e.g. fixed capital and inventories) might also be calculated where relevant to the particular programming problem.
[58]See supra, pp. 42-43.

Another requirement for an analytical technique appropriate to the needs of investment programming in underdeveloped areas is that it should include consideration of resource availabilities and prices (or "weights") in arriving at decisions. The conjunction of (a) a different resource pattern and (b) a different and wider array of technological alternatives available to the underdeveloped areas in contrast to those which existed during the development and structuring of the Western economies, together suggest that the character of capital formation required in the newly developing areas may be quite different from that of Western experience. Techniques for determining optimum investment programs and patterns must explicitly provide for consideration of resource "weighting" and technological variability, if they are to accord with the needs of public investment programming in underdeveloped areas today.

Closely related to Professor Leontief's technique is a method currently being applied by various public and private organizations active in the field of operations research, which goes by the forbidding names of "parametric" or "linear" or "mathematical" programming.[59] Although the names approach the occult, the essential concepts behind the techniques are more understandable. Basically, linear programming is a mathematical technique for determining the optimum utilization of given resources (e.g. capital, labor and materials) by reference to process or technological alternatives, and to the effect of relative scarcities of the factors on process choices. Given four sets of data, linear programming can determine a particular optimum solution for the use of stipulated resources.[60]

Applied to the development context, these four sets of data are: (a) the technical coefficients of production, as previously defined, showing the technological alternatives available for producing each desired commodity; (b) the program objectives—i.e. the production targets to be reached or the bill-of-goods to be maximized (where relative commodity prices are given); (c) the weights or "scarcity prices" showing the relative prices or policy-determined values to be accorded the factors expressed in the technical coefficients, so that the higher weighted factor will be used as sparingly and

[59]In the summary treatment which follows, several conversations with members of the staff of the RAND Corporation have been relied on as well as a few staff papers which they made available and a few published articles, the most intelligible of which was by Professor Dorfman of the University of California. See Dorfman, R., "Mathematical or Linear Programming," *American Economic Review*, Dec. 1953. Needless to say, for the idea that linear programming techniques and models may be relevant to investment programming problems in underdeveloped areas, and for any mistakes in presentation, the sources consulted do not share responsibility.

[60]What follows has been adapted from Moore, F. T. "An application of Linear Programming to the Determination of Requirements for Critical Materials used in Alloy Steels" U. S. Department of the Interior, Bureau of Mines, Feb. 1953.

the lower weighted factors as widely as are consistent with the program objectives; (d) any special program conditions or "constraints" as, for example, the condition that a minimum of a certain commodity or service must be produced in the final bill of goods, or a maximum of all or some of the weighted factors must be used in meeting (maximizing) the program.

With these data given, the linear programming technique, which can be mechanically applied by data-processing machines developed for the purpose, will determine the optimum method for producing the stipulated program. The optimum solution should minimize "cost," within the context of the coefficients, weights, constraints, and program objectives. The solution should show the needed pattern and quantities of resources and resource combinations, and, in the process, the needed quantity and kinds of capital formation which achievement of the stipulated program requires.

From the operational standpoint, the major difficulty in the use of linear programming in development planning lies in the problem of data: data concerning the coefficients, data concerning the program objectives, factor weights and program constraints. On an aggregative, economy-wide basis such data are unlikely to be available or assimilable within any reasonable time period in the underdeveloped countries. The data may, however, be manageable and obtainable for an individual sector, or for a particular region of the economy. On a sectoral, rather than national level, this approach might, for the first time, give developing countries improved tools for determining quantitative answers to such questions, for example, as the extent to which investment should be directed toward increasing output of wheat or corn; and the relative emphasis that should be accorded high dams, low dams, irrigation wells, land clearance, and fertilizer manufacture and use, as alternative aspects of increasing food production, in the investment of any given amount of capital.

These are very important and practical questions facing developing countries today. They are now normally answered in terms of unarticulated and imprecise assumptions as to program "balance," to the frequent detriment of economic development in the countries concerned. Further elaboration and application of linear programming techniques in the underdeveloped areas could have a tangible benefit in defining investment patterns which are optimal from the standpoint of the explicit program objectives of the countries concerned.

THE IDEA OF "LEADING GROWTH" SECTORS

Another idea, recently advanced by Walt Rostow of the Massachusetts Institute of Technology, deserves mention because of its direct relevance to the problem of "optimizing" investment in underdeveloped areas. Viewing the development process in the light of economic history, Professor Rostow notes that "at particular periods, different sectors have played a strategic role in determining the over-all growth rates of economies." [61] The fact that railroad development in the West played a particularly strategic role in initiating over-all growth in the American economy in the latter half of the 19th century is familiar enough. It is also generally accepted that similar initiative roles were played in subsequent periods in American development by the steel industry, the chemical, automotive, and electrical industries.

Rostow's point is that in analysing economic growth, one is struck by the similar roles played by different industries or sectors at different times and in different countries in *leading* the growth process. He suggests that the sectors of a growing economy may be usefully classified into three groups: the "primary" or leading growth sectors; "supplementary" growth sectors; and derived growth sectors, where growth occurs as a sort of by-product of the growth of such aggregates as population, national income, etc. The growth of food production in relation to population growth is an obvious example of derived growth.

Willard Thorp and other experts at a Merrill Center Conference expressed essentially the same view in terms of the historical role of certain specific investments in "triggering" a process of cumulative capital formation and growth. Leonard Rist of the International Bank also had this idea in mind in suggesting that it would be highly instructive to study in detail the inter-industry impact, over time and in particular areas where active development has ensued, of a specific new industrial undertaking. Calling attention to the case of Monterey in Mexico, Rist suggested a study of what has been a rapid over-all growth initiated by the establishment, forty years ago, of a brewery, which created a demand for glass making, bottlemaking, metal working and stamping for tin caps, and construction, and had fairly rapid and extensive effects throughout the local economy!

The point has direct and important bearing on the problems of economic development and investment programming in the underdeveloped countries today. If particular sectors play a peculiarly generative role in sparking a process of overall growth in the economy, it obviously will pay the developing countries to direct capital formation, as well as resource utilization generally, toward the leading sectors. These will be the sectors which will generate demand for supplementary products and services, and thereby serve both to induce further capital formation and to stimulate entrepreneurship.

Professor Rostow's idea raises several questions. For the leading sector concept to be useful in programming, it will be necessary to devise criteria

[61]Rostow, W. W. "Trends in the Allocation of Resources in Secular Growth," Center for International Studies, M. I. T., Unpublished Paper, Cambridge, 1953.

and methods for predicting which sectors are likely to play the leading sector role in the development of presently underdeveloped countries. The objective does not assume predictability of cyclical fluctuations in demand and supply nationally or internationally. The leading sector idea refers to the sequence and inter-industry causation in secular growth after cyclical fluctuations have been smoothed out of the growth pattern.

A more systematic analysis of the historical incidence of leading sectors and their correlation with certain economic circumstances would probably shed light on criteria and techniques of prediction. These circumstances, one would expect, would lie in a particular confluence among natural resources, technological innovation, population growth and the structure of demand in the economy, together combining, for example, to make the Western railroads in the late 19th century or the cotton textile industry at the end of the 18th century leading sectors in the growth of the U. S. and British economies respectively.

If the leading sector thesis is valid, and if techniques of predictability can be devised, the consideration of an optimum investment pattern would be markedly advanced. This addition might provide a program element or a "constraint" relating the optimum investment in year 1, 2 and 3 not only to given short-term output objectives, but also to the supplementary and derived investments stimulated in a subsequent period.

If leading sectors can be defined, there is the problem of reconciling the planned "direction" of resources to these sectors with the need for maintaining sufficient flexibility in the allocation of resources to permit the "supplementary" and "derived" consequences to work themselves out. This problem is inherent in any attempt to "plan" or program on the basis of a process which, historically, occurred autonomously.[62]

Program Possibilities and Research Needs. By comparison with the discussion of entrepreneurship, and the demand for capital, the preceding analysis of the problem of "optimizing" investment, has stressed theoretical, methodological and data considerations to a greater extent. In the following evaluation, greater attention will be devoted to research needs than program possibilities. Consideration of "optimization" techniques, generally, has not yet been extended to the context of underdeveloped areas. Consequently, there is need for a development of theory, technique and data *before* the program possibilities in this sphere can be better defined. This fact should not obscure the highly practical focus of research in this

---

[62]It should be noted that the idea of leading sectors as here used implicitly involves the notion of propagating free-enterprise responses to a given cluster of the "right" kinds of public investment.

field. As already noted, the broad problem of capital formation in under-developed areas is as much a problem of forming the right *kinds* of capital as it is of forming a specified *quantity* of capital in the aggregate.

PROGRAM POSSIBILITIES

The previous discussion noted that one major development in current economic thinking involved a view of technological change as an "endo-genous" and controllable factor. This view suggests the desirability of pro-gram measures which seek to institutionalize and regularize technological change in the underdeveloped countries. Such measures should induce ac-ceptance of the idea of adopting known, but untried, methods of produc-tion, as well as focussing attention on the possibility of making further im-provements in production methods in the course of adoption.

In nearly all of the underdeveloped countries in the Near East and Asia, emphasis is being placed on building an effective extension service to per-form this function in the field of agriculture. There is a plain need for a parallel function in small industry through the creation of an industrial extension service. The industrial extension service should be backed up by research "institutes," to provide new, or to adapt existing, production tech-niques to particular resource, skill, locational and marketing problems en-countered by the extension workers. The combination of extension meth-ods and institutionalized research facilities permits the introduction of improved small industry techniques and the devising of new techniques which accord with the particular country situation.

This is, of course, familiar in agriculture. It is generally neglected, how-ever, in such typical small industry fields as ceramics, woodworking, metal working, brick working, bicycle manufacture and assembly, and weaving. Indonesia has pioneered in this field and its industrial inspection service, and expanding network of research institutes and producers' cooperatives in the small industry field are perhaps farther advanced than any compara-ble development in the Near East and Asia generally. A program to set up in Indonesia a regional training center, so that administrative and technical personnel from the neighboring countries might study Indonesia's methods and experience in this field, would be a significant step toward the end of raising the productivity of existing capital and new capital formation in the underdeveloped areas.[63]

[63]As a supplement to this program, a plan suggested by Dr. C. M. Vakil, Director of the Bombay School of Economics and Sociology, for accelerating technological improvement in small industry, is worth noting. Though conceived in terms of India's own problems in this field, it has more general applicability to other countries as well. Vakil's plan would start with a basic economic and technical survey of small industries in India in terms of their character, number, location, productivity, etc. The survey would be conducted by such Indian research organizations as the Bombay and Delhi Schools, with foreign assist-

RESEARCH NEEDS

Special stress was placed in the foregoing analysis on the need to select from available technological alternatives those which would maximize productivity of existing capital and of new capital formation. The first requirement for implementing this approach is a selective study of comparative technologies. Such a study would represent a quantitative appraisal of the different methods used in the production of certain basic industries in different countries. The basic industries would be those whose roles in development programs are typically prominent, e.g. food production and processing, textiles, building materials and construction, woodwork, ceramics, metallurgical industry, agricultural machinery, etc. The different methods used in these industries would be analyzed in terms of capital utilization, locational scatter or concentration, size of plant, and utilization of skilled and unskilled labor. An inventory of technical coefficients for each of these criteria would be drawn up indicating the range of alternatives for the various industries.[64] The different countries would be those with a presumed diversity of technology and might, for example, comprise Japan, a Scandinavian country and the United States.

Granted the serious statistical, definitional and organizational problems of an economic-engineering study of comparative technology, the need is great. The results would be an important element in determining the fields or industries in which capital formation should be concentrated, and the methods of production appropriate to a particular country from the array of available technological alternatives.

The "productivity" programs of the Foreign Operations Administration in its European and Latin American activities indicate that frequently a change in organizational and management techniques, especially in the area of management-labor relations, can have as significant an effect on the productivity of a given quantity of capital as a change in the technological process of production. Presumably, the effect of an innovation in management techniques would be measureable through an alteration in

---

ance and participation as appropriate. On the basis of the survey, the participating institutions would formulate specific problems connected with the production and marketing of small industry products. These problems would then be turned over to the existing technology institutes in India. (The existing institutes apparently are well-equipped and staffed but have directed their attention toward "basic," long-term scientific research. Vakil's plan would involve a redirection of their attention to more immediate production and operating problems.) The results uncovered by the technological institutes would then be incorporated in small industry improvement programs under India's Five Year Plan.

[64] See Bohr, op. cit. Bohr concentrates more on the differences among industries in a given country. The approach suggested here involved differences among different countries in methods of production in a given industry.

the ratio between capital and output, or labor and output. In the course of the study of comparative technology already suggested, an effort should be made to identify and measure cases where technically similar processes are associated with a differential productivity of capital and labor, due to varying organizational and management techniques. An appraisal of alternative organizational and management techniques is related to an appraisal of technological alternatives. Together such paired studies might provide useful data for helping underdeveloped countries to maximize the productivity of existing and new capital formation.

Reference has been made to the recent development of econometric techniques for determining optimum program decisions for a variety of production problems in the United States. The use of these "linear" programming techniques has not been extended to problems of underdeveloped areas. However, the essential ingredients of mathematical programming and of public investment programming in underdeveloped areas are the same. These ingredients comprise: (a) a quantitative specification of program objectives, i.e., production or income goals, as well as any special limitations imposed on the program, (for example, that a stipulated amount of new employment opportunities must be created by the program); (b) the technological alternatives—expressed in terms of technical coefficients reflecting the various ways that capital and other productive factors can be combined in producing the program called for; and (c) the different weights or "prices" to be assigned the factors expressed in (b). Given these data, the technique can help select a single pattern of resource utilization, including the required pattern of capital formation, which will be the optimum program under the stated assumptions. Theoretically, this method can provide a means for guiding public investment in underdeveloped areas into those fields where it will have the greatest effect.

In practice, application of this method to economic development problems will be limited by the shortage of data. The comparative technological studies already referred to will provide valuable data for use in a limited application of linear programming to problems of economic development. However, in view of both the limitations of data and the need to adapt the method to a new context, it would be desirable to test this method on a limited sectoral basis in one of the underdeveloped countries before it is more broadly applied. The services of operations research groups familiar with this technique might be usefully invoked to assure that the new effort draws fully on already accumulated experience.

The preceding analysis referred to the peculiar role of different economic sectors in "leading" the growth process in different countries at different times. Historically, the important role of such leading sectors suggests the need for formulating criteria which will permit prediction of sectors likely to play an analogous role in the next decade or generation in presently underdeveloped countries. Plainly, if the potentially leading sectors can be predicted, the framing of an optimum program of both private and public capital formation would be greatly facilitated. At the same time, if the determination of key sectors is accurate, capital accumulation and growth should be able to proceed more as an organic and self-generating process and less as a system of imposed controls.

Two analogous approaches might be suggested for testing and analyzing the "leading sector" concept and, hopefully, for formulating criteria which will permit the prediction of potentially leading sectors in newly developing countries.

A systematic analysis of the historical incidence of leading sectors and their correlation with certain prevailing economic circumstances (e.g. resource discovery, technological innovation, evidence of shifting demand patterns) would be one approach. This approach would, for example, try to answer the question, "What was there in the economic situation of England and the world generally in the late 18th century that would have made the prospective leading sector role of the cotton textiles industry predictable?"

Another approach to the problem of inter-industry sequence and causality would involve a current field study or case analysis of a particular rapidly-growing region in a presently or recently underdeveloped country. To the extent possible, such a study would seek to construct an intertemporal as well as inter-industry model of the region concerned. The field study would try to measure the sequence and rate at which economic activities in the rapidly developing region have grown. This would be related to particular characteristics of the region's economic situation at the start of and during the growth process. Dealing with current and recently past data, this approach might confront fewer data limitations, and might permit a closer investigation, than the historical approach. Monterey, Mexico, the Damodar Valley development in India, or the São Paulo area of Brazil might be suggested as suitable cases for testing this approach.

CHAPTER FOUR

FOREIGN INVESTMENT AND CAPITAL FORMATION

The Problem. The subject of foreign investment has perhaps generated more discussion and fewer effective results than any other aspect of the problem of capital formation in underdeveloped areas. American private investment abroad in the period 1945-1952 has, in the aggregate, totaled $9.3 billion, including reinvestment of earnings. On an annual basis, private investment abroad has been near the peak of the 1920's with the significant differences: (1) that post World War II investment has been almost entirely in the form of direct investment rather than the portfolio investment which characterized the 1920's; (2) that the current rate of investment is considerably below the level of the 1920's in real terms, and represents a much smaller fraction of American national income than in the earlier period. Of the total, almost 40 per cent has been invested in Canada, 30 per cent in Latin America, 15 per cent in Western Europe and dependencies, and 15 per cent in the rest of the world including the Near East and Asian region under consideration in this paper. The bulk of the latter is accounted for by investments of petroleum companies in the Near East. There has been little tendency for American private capital to invest in the Near East and Asia other than in "extractive" industry, such as petroleum, for which there is a ready, existing dollar market. There are apparently no signs of a substantial change from this pattern.

In most of the general discussion of foreign investment, attention has been concentrated on the broader economic and political-economic reasons for the pattern and quantity of American foreign investment in the post war period. In a recent study of factors limiting American private foreign investments, for example, the Department of Commerce stressed four broad reasons for the generally unfavorable investment "climate" abroad:[65]

[65]"Study of Factors Limiting American Private Foreign Investment,"—*Summary of Preliminary Findings and Recommendations,* Dept. of Commerce, July 1953, p. 5.

(a) the imbalance and dislocation in trade and currency relationships leading to controls over the amounts of and purposes for which capital may be invested and the rate at which earnings and capital may be repatriated;

(b) economic nationalism in the underdeveloped countries accompanied by unfavorable reactions on the part of the public and domestic business, and by an increasing stringency and number of controls by governments over the entry and conduct of foreign investments;

(c) insecure and unstable political and social conditions which cause uncertainties and lack of confidence on the part of investors;

(d) low levels of economic development as reflected in inadequate basic facilities, shortage of trained labor, lack of allied industries and shortage of local venture capital.

There is no doubt that these general factors affect the climate for foreign investment, and it is equally clear that the "climate" affects the behavior of investors. However, it may be suggested that the Commerce Department study, the reports of the Randall Commission, and of the earlier Rockefeller, Gray and Bell groups as well, have devoted too little attention to the specifics of investment opportunities. It may be more fruitful to try to identify whether and what specific investment opportunities exist, rather than to generalize on the climatic obstacles to investment.

In seeking to relate foreign investment to capital formation in underdeveloped areas, several points might be noted.

The extent to which the capital needs of the underdeveloped countries are likely to be met by private foreign investment is exceedingly limited. Historically, the role of foreign investment in economic development has not been large relative to total domestic capital formation, even under the most favorable circumstances. British investment in American railroads in the 19th century gave a significant impetus to American growth because of the particular form of the investment, not because it was large in relation to total net capital formation. Even in the more recent case of Canadian development, in which private investment from abroad has been large, the contribution of capital inflow to domestic capital formation was quantitatively less than Canada's export of domestic capital.

Currently, there are several reasons why large quantities of private investment from abroad are *not* likely to be available for meeting the internal capital requirements of the underdeveloped areas. Reference has already been made to the strong tendency of American investors to concentrate on dollar export or "outward-flow" products.[66] These are not the industries in

[66]See Block, Ernest: "U. S. Foreign Investment and the Dollar Shortage," *Review of Economics and Statistics,* May 1953; also Sufrin, S. C., "Foreign Investment," *Foreign Policy Bulletin,* Sept. 1953.

which the bulk of the unsatisfied capital needs of the Asian and Near Eastern countries lie.

Another reason lies in the relatively high rates of return which American investors are able to realize from domestic investment or foreign investment in closer and more familiar areas than the Near East and Asia.[67] The frequent image of the American investor, as one who continually and actively is looking for prospects of high returns in any field, however remote geographically or technically, is probably fanciful. Putting it another way, it is likely that the American investor places an unusually high risk discount on the expected returns from investments in new and remote areas, such as the Near East and Asia. Henry Aubrey has called attention to the influence of precedent and risk-discounting on decision-making by domestic entrepreneurs in underdeveloped areas.[68] Lack of precedent is an equally important obstacle to expanded foreign investment in the Near East and Asia. In other words, prospective American investors' calculations of risk, and their attendant discount of anticipated earnings, will tend to be high for unfamiliar countries and situations.

It is also probably true that American investment, especially portfolio investment, is more likely to follow rather than lead economic development in the Near East and South and Southeast Asia. Hence, it is unlikely that such investment can be counted on to make any large quantitative contribution to bridging investment-gaps which national development programs estimate as necessary for getting development under way.

The foregoing discussion has suggested that prospective American investment in the underdeveloped areas is likely to be quantitatively small in relation to total capital requirements. Nevertheless, it can be a significant marginal factor as a means of "triggering" indigenous capital formation. The Sears Roebuck experience in Mexico has already been noted. Although exact figures are not available in the National Planning Association study, it is reasonable to infer from the study that the original Sears' investment acted as a major stimulant to local capital formation in the shops and plants which were created or expanded to supply Sears' market outlets.

---

[67]Discussions with several private investment groups suggest that the strong demand for corporate investment funds within the U. S.—due both to the established practice of internal-financing of corporate investment and to the high level at which the American economy has been functioning generally—is a major deterrent to corporate interest in foreign investment. In this context, it is possible that a modest "adjustment" in the American economy, sufficient to reduce somewhat the demand for corporate investment funds at home but not sufficient to reduce substantially over-all corporate net earnings, might have a buoyant effect on investment abroad.

[68]Aubrey, H. *Industrial Enterprise in Underdeveloped Countries,* National Bureau of Economic Research, 1953, p. 14.

While it may be assumed that a partial explanation for the possible triggering role of foreign investment lies in the acceleration of indigenous demand, this is not the only explanation. That direct investment includes management as well as capital is too well known to warrant elaboration here. By providing training facilities, and the important ingredient of precedent, direct foreign investment can be especially important as a catalyst to indigenous entrepreneurial activity and, consequently, to accelerated capital formation.

Notwithstanding the emphasis placed by the Department of Commerce on the prevalence and adverse effects of "economic nationalism" in discouraging foreign investment, there are signs that this attitude is abating.[69] Though policy statements are frequently a long way from action measures, there have been indications that the underdeveloped countries in this region are becoming increasingly interested in attracting foreign investment.[70] Complementing this change in attitude is a growing understanding by American business interests of the desirability of providing training facilities and management opportunities for local personnel in foreign ventures.[71]

Mention has already been made of the question whether or not profitable investment opportunities exist in the underdeveloped countries. It has frequently been argued that profitable investment opportunities should generally be expected to exist in underdeveloped areas since these areas are typically poor in capital and rich in labor and other resources,[72] and hence the marginal productivity of capital tends to be high.

On the other hand, it has also been argued that specific profitable opportunities for foreign investment do not exist or are exceedingly limited. This contention is made because the lack of such social overhead as power, transport and communication facilities results in such high initial fixed costs to the firm as to offset the high anticipated productivity of scarce capital. Hence, it is argued, notably by Dr. Hans Singer and others, that the process of investment in underdeveloped areas is discontinuous, and the

---

[69]See Wolf, C. "Some Reflections on the Status of Economic Development in South and Southeast Asia," *Economic Development and Cultural Change,* October 1953, pp. 207-8.
[70]See, for example, the statement by India's Minister of Commerce and Industry in Parliament, April 4, 1953, on the need to attract foreign capital, and the government's press announcement of March 3, 1953 that exchange restrictions on repatriation of capital have been removed to permit repatriation of both principle and appreciation in the value of investment.
[71]The experience of the American Cyanamid Company's participation in the Atul Products plant near Bombay is an especially interesting example of a growing understanding among American industrialists of the requirements for successful ventures in this region. See Monthly News Bulletin, American Cyanamid Company, May 1952.
[72]See, for example, Nurkse, R., op. cit., p. 130.

potentially high marginal productivity of capital cannot be realized until massive investments in overhead facilities are completed.

The theoretical view that profitable opportunities do exist seems to be supported by the findings of a survey in 1951 conducted by the National Industrial Conference Board of American businesses with investments abroad.[73] The Board's survey covered 107 companies holding an estimated 54 per cent of total American direct investment abroad. Of these companies, 89 per cent did *not* believe that the lack of profit prospects, commensurate with risks abroad and with profit opportunities at home, was a major obstacle to investment abroad. As stated in the Board's findings:

> It does seem clear that opportunities for profit exist abroad. Foreign investment does not appear to be limited because of the absence of profit opportunities.[74]

There is some quantitative information which, though admittedly inconclusive, would seem to corroborate the Board's findings. In 1950, the last year for which the Department of Commerce has published a census of U. S. direct investments abroad, the net worth of U. S. direct investments in India, Pakistan, Indonesia and the Philippines was $227 million. Net earnings of these investments *before* taxes were estimated at $133 million or about 58 per cent of net worth.[75] By comparison, the net earnings of 1800 of the leading manufacturing corporations within the U. S. in 1951 and 1952 were, before taxes, estimated at 33 per cent and 27 per cent, respectively.[76]

Too much should not be inferred from these figures. The net worth of U. S. investments in the four countries cited is probably considerably understated due to war-time write-offs. Moreover, the frequent practice of treating rehabilitation costs, e.g. of refineries, plantations, etc., as current operating expenses rather than new investment, also tends to lower the net worth figure. Despite these important qualifications, the figures at least suggest that a more careful study is warranted of the profitability of existing foreign investments in underdeveloped areas and the specific opportunities that exist for an expansion of such investments.

Up to this point various aspects of private American investment in underdeveloped areas have been considered in relation to capital requirements and public attitudes within these countries. Brief mention will also be made of the relation between private investment abroad and U. S. public policy.

---

[73]*Obstacles to Direct Foreign Investment,* National Industrial Conference Board, 1951.
[74]cf. supra, pp. 19-20, although the existence of opportunities for profitable investment of indigenous capital does not necessarily imply that the inducements will be adequate to attract foreign investment.
[75]*Direct Private Foreign Investments of the United States,* Census of 1950, U. S. Department of Commerce, November, 1953, p. 51, 53.
[76]National City Bank *Monthly Letter on Business and Economic Conditions,* New York, April, 1953, p. 42.

In addition to the standard Friendship, Commerce and Navigation Treaties, designed to assure non-discriminatory treatment for American investors, two policy instrumentalities bearing directly on the stimulation of foreign investment might be noted. The first concerns the use of investment guarantees to insure foreign investors against the risk of expropriation and inconvertibility of capital and earnings. In view of the emphasis placed by both the Department of Commerce and National Industrial Conference Board studies on restrictions of remittances and capital movements, and, to a lesser extent, on expropriation, as barriers to foreign investment, one might expect that U. S. government guarantees, covering these risks, would be oversubscribed. Actually, application for guarantees have been surprisingly few and only about 25 per cent of the $200 million in guarantee coverage authorized by Congress in 1948-1950 has been used up to the summer of 1954.

This apparent anomaly may be partly accounted for by the time that is required for a program of this kind to get underway. In part, it may also be due to the limited extent of risk coverage which is confined to a maximum of 170 per cent of the original dollar investment and which is itself further reduced as remittances are successfully made through regular channels. To some extent, the failure of business to apply for guarantees may also be due to the fact that existing guarantee authority does not cover some risks which deter foreign investment e.g. devaluation, war damage, political instability, etc. Notwithstanding these partial explanations, the actual reasons for the disappointing showing of investment guarantees are not too clear and warrant more detailed study, along lines that will be suggested below.

A second public instrumentality for influencing foreign investment is tax policy. All of the recent studies of foreign investment have touched on this subject and the President's 1954 Budget Message to the Congress made several recommendations for more favorable tax treatment to income from foreign investment.[77] Although the arguments on both sides of this question tend to be vigorous, it is extremely hazardous to predict the probable quantitative effects on foreign investment in the underdeveloped areas of preferential tax treatment on income from such investment. There is no doubt that the tax moratorium in Puerto Rico has been a major inducement to capital inflow. And it is likely that the 14 per cent reduction in corporate tax rate, for firms doing more than 95 per cent of their business in countries of the Western Hemisphere[78] other than the United States, has been a significant stimulus to investment in Latin America. However, it is not clear to what extent this investment might have occurred apart from these tax

[77]*Congressional Record*, Vol. 100, No. 11, January 21, 1954, Page 550.
[78]Under the Western Hemisphere Trade Corporation Act.

inducements. Tax remissions on income from foreign investment might be simply a subsidy to one particular investment group rather than a quantitatively significant stimulus to economic development. There is a need here for more precise study of what might be termed the "tax elasticity" of foreign investment in underdeveloped areas, or the probable effect of a given percentage reduction in corporate tax rates on the percentage increase in foreign investment (in particular areas).

The relationships between foreign investment and indigenous capital formation have, up to this point, been discussed only in gross terms. No attempt has been made, for example, to distinguish between the different forms which foreign investment can take, or the relative effect on indigenous capital formation of foreign investment in the form of capital goods imports as against payments for local labor or materials. Direct investment in capital goods clearly adds to the productive capital stock, while foreign investment in local materials or services normally makes available "free" foreign exchange which may be dissipated in consumers goods imports. However, it is theoretically possible, though perhaps not likely, that capital goods imports financed through foreign investment may simply substitute for capital imports that otherwise would have taken place, and hence may not appreciably add to the stock of available capital. It is also possible, and perhaps more likely, that foreign investment which makes "free" exchange available for consumers goods imports, may have a major and multiple effect on internal capital formation. In many cases, for example, idle resources exist in the underdeveloped areas, but their mobilization is prevented by the anticipated balance of payments repercussion that would ensue from using them. In such cases, the availability of marginal "free" exchange, as a result of foreign investment in local materials or labor, can permit an expansion in internal capital formation beyond the amount of the original investment.

In southern Italy the relationship between a given amount of "free" foreign exchange, and the expansion in internal capital formation that it would make possible, has been worked out in considerable detail, and has in fact been the basis for a recent loan by the International Bank to finance consumers goods imports as a means of carrying out an internal investment program.[79] Briefly stated, the determination of the relationship between internal capital formation and "induced" import requirements, involves the following steps: (1) a technical analysis of the proposed investment to determine the factor inputs, in terms both of kinds and costs, which will be locally required; (2) an analysis, largely by the use of data on family bud-

[79]"Economic Effects of an Investment Program in Southern Italy," *SVIMEZ*, Rome, 1951. We are indebted to Dr. Rosenstein-Rodan of M. I. T. for mentioning this case.

gets, of the expenditure patterns of recipients of local currency paid out under (1) above, in order to estimate the income-generating effect of such expenditures. This analysis involves a study of income leakages through savings, taxes and imports in order to determine the income effect of a specific dose of additional domestic investment; (3) an estimate of the ratio of induced imports to increased income, i.e., the marginal propensity to import as derived from existing statistics on income-import relations.

By a combination of these steps, it was possible in the case of southern Italy to determine the extent to which a stipulated amount of foreign exchange, primarily for consumers goods imports, would permit a multiple expansion of internal capital formation.

The foregoing model may have direct bearing on the problem of capital formation in underdeveloped areas insofar as public grants-in-aid for economic development may be likely to take the form of surplus agricultural commodities rather than capital goods. If this turns out to be the trend of American public investment, or "foreign aid," in the underdeveloped areas, it will become a matter of considerable practical as well as theoretical importance to determine the extent to which such surpluses may be properly used as a lever for raising internal capital formation.

Program Possibilities and Research Needs.

PROGRAM POSSIBILITIES

Reference has already been made to the theoretical arguments that can be adduced, on the one hand, in support of the proposition that profitable opportunities for foreign investment should exist in the underdeveloped areas, and, on the other hand, that they cannot be expected to exist until after a massive investment in social overhead has been completed. At the same time, brief mention was also made of the fact that businessmen themselves apparently do not believe that a major obstacle to foreign investment lies in the absence of profitable investment opportunities.

While argumentation has proceeded as to whether profitable opportunities for foreign investment exist in underdeveloped areas, most public policy attention in this field has been focussed on the broader issues of investment "climate" rather than on the specifics of investment situations.

Probably the most important contribution that can be made in this field lies in moving from the realm of the general to the specific by defining and documenting a limited number of concrete opportunities for foreign investment in several of the larger underdeveloped countries of the Near East, and South and Southeast Asia. Essentially what would be involved would be the preparation of selected investment prospectuses which would attempt to pinpoint the five or six outstanding opportunities for foreign investment in such countries as Egypt, India, Burma, and Indonesia. These prospectuses would concentrate on the compilation and evaluation of the basic cost and market data for each such investment situation, including data on labor costs, processing costs, transportation costs, and local markets, regional markets, national markets and export markets.

Prospectuses of this kind are necessary not only to test concretely the question whether attractive opportunities for foreign investment exist, but also to elicit definite reactions from prospective American investors. Nevertheless, it is apparently not likely that government authorities in either the United States or in the underdeveloped countries themselves are at this stage likely to undertake the financing of a project of this kind. It also seems doubtful that financing for such an exploratory venture can be expected from private business organizations in the United States. It would therefore seem appropriate for a private non-profit Foundation to break ground in this field. Such an undertaking might involve the services of a major, reputable American financial firm to prepare the prospectuses on a direct contract basis with payments confined to meeting services costs, or, alternatively, might take the form of a contract by a host government and an American financial firm with private Foundation support for the contract. Clearly, an effort of this kind would require an invitation from the host country government.

Brief reference has already been made to the important role which foreign investment in the underdeveloped areas can play not only in providing capital but in providing management services as well. Many of the underdeveloped countries have both political and economic reasons for desiring and needing management services, even without capital participation. There are two specific ways in which preliminary program action might help to facilitate an increase in the use of foreign management services in internal capital ventures. The first would be through the preparation of an inventory of the different kinds of management and technical services that are available and have been provided to underdeveloped countries throughout the world independently of capital participation. Such an inventory would catalog, for the use of the underdeveloped countries, the kinds of management services they can readily secure in connection with public investment projects. Secondly, an analysis might be made of the different kinds of foreign management contracts that have been negotiated in various countries, together with an evaluation of the contractual forms that have been or may be devised for reconciling the interests of the host country in benefiting from foreign management and training while retaining ultimate control, with the interests of the foreign management group in securing adequate operational authority without financial commitment.

RESEARCH NEEDS

In discussing specific instrumentalities of public policy which are available for stimulating foreign investment, both investment guarantees and tax policy have been mentioned. As already noted the recent studies of the Department of Commerce and the National Industrial Conference Board placed major emphasis on the inhibiting effect on foreign investment of restrictions on capital movements and remittances of profits. In view of the fact that the guarantee authority which the Congress has conferred on the Executive Branch would seem to insure against these particular kinds of risks, it would seem advisable to undertake a study of why investment guarantees have not been more widely used or widely demanded by prospective American investors. Does the reason for the limited use of investment guarantees lie in the limitations hitherto placed on the maximum coverage of guarantee contracts? Or is the reason basically to be found in the fact that guarantees against inconvertibility and expropriation do not really deal with the risks which bother prospective investors? In this connection, it would be desirable to ascertain the thinking of the business community itself in relation to guarantees and how they might be modified to be more effective.

In this field of tax policy, different views have been expressed concerning the probable effect on foreign investment of partial or total remission of taxes on foreign income. In this connection a systematic study should be made of the quantitative effect of the 14 per cent reduction in tax rates, under the Western Hemisphere Trade Corporation Act, on the percentage increase in American private investment in Latin America, and of the particular kinds of investment that have been most responsive to this adjustment. Such a study might shed some light on the tax elasticity of foreign investment.

The interest elasticity of demand for and supply for foreign portfolio investment might also be investigated empirically, as another potentially useful adjunct of public policy. It is likely that underdeveloped countries sometimes hold back requests for loans, e.g. from the International or Export-Import Banks, because of the real or anticipated burden of servicing portfolio indebtedness if an adverse shift in their balances of payments occurs. If the probable effect of a given reduction in interest rates on portfolio investment could be appraised and were found to be significant, it might be possible to devise public policy instruments for subsidizing interest rates on such investments without either disturbing international money markets, or leading to arbitrage. For example, under such an arrangement, a prospective institutional or other lender might receive interest of perhaps 5 or 6 per cent, and a prospective underdeveloped-area borrower might pay interest of perhaps 2 per cent. A public subsidy by the

U. S. government, for example, might make up the difference between the two rates. Subsidized interest rates might thus serve to increase the availability of loanable portfolio funds and the demand for such funds in underdeveloped countries. Granted the precaution that would need to be taken to prevent abuse, such a device might be a useful alternative to direct U. S. government grants.

The potential importance of surplus agricultural commodities, as a vehicle for public "investment" in the underdeveloped countries, has already been noted. Given the existence of idle resources and idle productive capacity in particular underdeveloped countries, it may be possible to relate the use of U. S. agricultural surpluses to a multiple expansion of internal capital formation, without causing inflation. An investigation of the probable scope of this "multiplier" concept would require an application of the analytical technique already used in southern Italy, to particular countries of the Near East and South and Southeast Asia. Some attention is being given to this problem in the Executive Branch, but the more detailed analysis (e.g., of factor inputs associated with particular investment projects, of marginal consumption propensities, and induced demand for imports), which is needed to apply the multiplier principle to underdeveloped areas, may require additional research and fact-finding.

CHAPTER FIVE

OTHER RESEARCH NEEDS

THE FOREGOING STATEMENT has not purported to be an exhaustive treatment of all problems relating to capital formation in underdeveloped areas. Rather, it has attempted to block out three major problem areas in which important research needs and program possibilities exist. The first problem area emphasized the socio-economic elements involved in increasing the demand for capital and evoking indigenous entrepreneurship. The second section concentrated more on theory and research relating to the problem of developing analytical tools to determine the optimum pattern of investment in underdeveloped areas. The third section suggested the possible role of foreign investment in triggering indigenous capital formation and ways in which this role might be effectuated.

There are, of course, many other aspects of the broad problem of capital formation which might be considered. Two of these will be briefly noted in concluding.

Consideration of capital formation must at some point confront the harsh reality of population pressures and prospects in many of the underdeveloped countries. The writings of demographers on economic development sound a nearly uniform note of pessimism on prospects for "breaking through" the Malthusian population barrier.[80] In some countries, such as India, where the absolute rate of population increase is large, there is apparently no single answer to the population problem. Presumably the prospects for breaking through the Malthusian barrier lie in the growth of literacy, urbanization, organized birth control programs, and an initial jump in real income of sufficient magnitude to have an impact on living habits and birth rates.

[80]See, for example, Davis, Kingsley, "Population and Change in Underdeveloped Areas," *Columbia Journal of International Affairs,* Spring, 1950.

64

There are several ways in which these approaches to the population problem relate to the formation of capital. For example, the capital requirements connected with a substantial jump in real income would depend on the capital-output ratio connected with the particular investments that are made. As Dr. Kuznets has suggested, these capital-output coefficients seem to have varied considerably in the development of different countries in the past. Nevertheless, it would probably be illuminating to investigate for several countries the relationship between changing rates of capital formation on the one hand, and changes in birth rates, death rates, and population growth, on the other, in the experience of different countries historically. Such an investigation might suggest certain critical points in the capital-income curve in relation to impact on population growth.

Some writers have suggested that a diffusion of the gains in output realized by increased capital formation will only raise population in the underdeveloped countries; while others have emphasized the need for a wide distribution of the increments in output in the form of increased consumption in order to provide an incentive for a reduction in birth rates. It may be that these two views are not as inconsistent as they appear. Perhaps there is a "critical" size to the marginal increments in consumption which are required to alter established birth rates. Below this critical point, increments in consumption may simply tend to be eaten up by growth in population. This would seem to be another line of research which might be usefully pursued in relating the problem of capital formation to the broad issues of population pressures in underdeveloped countries.

Another way in which capital formation may be presumed to bear directly on the population problem lies in the differential effects of various forms and locations of new capital on rates of population growth. It is frequently suggested that urban concentration of capital tends to have a greater effect in reducing birth rates than the same amount of capital located in rural areas. Is this generally true or is it true only for certain areas? The answer to this type of question has important locational implications for investment programming in underdeveloped areas.

Another important problem requiring additional research is the relationship between commercial policy and capital formation in the underdeveloped countries. The division of thinking on this issue is quite sharp. On the one hand there is little question but that protectionist commercial policies have historically played a significant role in stimulating indigenous investment. It has also been suggested that protectionist measures tend to encourage foreign investment within the protected market as a means of avoiding quantitative restrictions or import taxes. Recent experience in Mexico and the Philippines is relevant in this connection: heavy quantitative restrictions in the former, and a 17 per cent foreign exchange tax in the latter, acted as fairly rapid stimuli both to internal capital formation and foreign capital inflow.

At the same time, and aside from the familiar infant-industry argument for protectionist measures, there is no doubt that for underdeveloped countries to invest scarce capital in fields which require a protected market is hardly justifiable if opportunities exist for investment in fields which have a comparative advantage over competing foreign producers. It is also probable that in some cases protectionist commercial policies may so adversely affect the expectations of potential foreign investors as to discourage new capital inflow and perhaps even to stimulate a flight of capital.

Without attempting to evaluate these differing views here, it would at least seem useful to investigate in some detail the historical relationship between various kinds of restrictive commercial policies and rates of indigenous capital formation and foreign investment. In such a study, a detailed analysis of recent experience in the Philippines and Mexico, and of other underdeveloped countries in different economic situations, would be especially significant.

PART THREE

MATERIALS CONSULTED AND
METHODS USED

CHAPTER SIX

ANNOTATED BIBLIOGRAPHY AND CURRENT RESEARCH

ONE PURPOSE of this report, as already noted, was to provide an annotated bibliography of selected literature dealing with particular aspects of economic development. Scholars, researchers, and both public and private administrators, it was felt, would benefit if some of the recent literature could be listed, arranged in some useful order and a brief description given of the contents. In a summary listing of this sort, critical or evaluative comment would be out of order because of the brief space allotted each item.

The output of the International Organizations (United Nations, Food and Agriculture Organization, and The International Bank for Reconstruction and Development) is so voluminous, that a special bibliography was prepared for reports and documents of these agencies.

The research output from other sources includes books, monographs, articles and reports of University research agencies, individual scholars, governments and business studies. A separate selected bibliography was prepared covering this literature. The Bibliography of International Organizations Publications is more complete than that of other books and periodicals.

PUBLICATIONS OF INTERNATIONAL ORGANIZATIONS

The orientation of the International Organization literature tends to be broad. Underdevelopment as a broad economic, cultural and social phenomenon, rather than the more selective orientation of capital formation, is the general concern of these Organizations. At the same time, various agencies of the United Nations publish reports on specific technical questions, e.g. technology in the coal industry, flood damage in Asia, etc. which are generally more detailed and sharper in focus than any other published research.

The International Organization bibliography was compiled after an examination of virtually all the printed and mimeographed material issued by the United Nations between the years 1947 and 1954. A full list of titles of such documents was secured from various United Nations catalogues and publication lists. Publications falling within the scope of underdeveloped areas, broadly defined, were examined and evaluated as to their relevance to this report. A brief explanatory paragraph was then prepared on each publication.

Similar investigations were made for publications of the International Bank for Reconstruction and Development (IBRD) and the Food and Agriculture Organization (FAO). These three Organizations are the ones mainly concerned with development problems.

Each listing contains title, sales number, price and place of publication of the document in question. Prices are given in dollars only, although other currencies are acceptable for purchases outside the United States. The studies and reports are usually available in English, French and Spanish.

Some of the documents recorded are mimeographed. Such documents are not for sale by the United Nations, but many may be secured directly from the United Nations in New York, or may be found at libraries which are depositories for United Nations materials and documents.

In addition to the date and place of publication, each title is followed by one or more bracketed letters. These letters are symbols indicating the relevance of the title in question to the check list-questionnaire which is reproduced in Appendix One—"The Questionnaire" on page 126. The letters used only record the major significance of the title in question with respect to the questionnaire. In most instances the subject matter of the document in question is broader than suggested by the classification letters. The notation "Entire Outline" means that the item under discussion considers all or virtually all aspects of the check list-questionnaire.

The bibliography is divided as follows:

Section 1. General. This section includes studies and reports which are classified into (a) International trade and arrangements, (b) technical assistance and economic development, (c) capital formation and economic development, (d) miscellaneous.

Section 2. Statistical. This includes all Annual Reports of the United Nations which are basically statistical in orientation. In this classification are included the Annual World Economic Reports, Supplements and Regional Reports.

Section 3. Regional. The United Nations publications reported here are divided into those dealing with (a) Africa, (b) Asia and the Far East, (c) Latin America, (d) the Middle East.

Section 4. Food and Agriculture Organization Reports. These are divided into (a) General and statistical studies which include all Annual Reports and Statistical Reports, (b) technical studies, (c) regional studies.

Section 5. International Bank for Reconstruction and Development. No sub-classification of these reports is required because each study is a report on a particular country.

(Within each classification, titles are arranged chronologically.)

BOOKS AND PERIODICALS

The second bibliographical section comprises a selected list of books and journal articles. This bibliography does not pretend to be exhaustive. Rather it is limited to selected work dealing with capital formation and foreign investment in underdeveloped areas and considered relevant to the present report by the authors. With few exceptions, only publications issued subsequent to 1949 were examined. Attention was directed toward material dealing with function and processes rather than with unique elements of a particular country situation. However, occasionally studies of particular countries have been included. Studies of South and Southeast Asia and the Near East constitute the major geographical interest of the selection.

As in the case of the International Organization bibliography, each title is followed by one or more bracketed letters. As noted previously, these letters are symbols indicating the relevance of the title in question to the questionnaire contained in Appendix One.

The listing is alphabetical by authors. This order of classification was resorted to as more practicable than a functional classification, since the spread of subject matter is less than in the preceding bibliography.

CURRENT RESEARCH

Both in the United States and abroad, there is a great interest in research on underdeveloped areas. A general statement on current research is to be found in Appendix One. It was felt, however, that persons and institutions concerned with economic development would be interested in a listing of current research being carried on by particular institutions or individuals. This knowledge may assist (1) in avoiding duplication, (2) in the exchange of ideas and data, and (3) in structuring the general area of investigation.

To these ends a third part was added to the bibliographical section dealing, if only partially, with research currently in process. This section describes research in progress, but does not refer to specific publications.

Again, as in the case of the two bibliographies, each research topic is followed by one or more bracketed letters, referring to the check list-questionnaire contained in Appendix One.

The reader desiring a detailed listing of current projects (and literature) on British Colonial matters is referred to the Colonial Social Science Research Council and Colonial Economic Research Committee Annual Reports. These excellent Reports are made to H. M. Secretary of State for the Colonies by a committee of outstanding scholars, social and business leaders, and may be secured from the British Colonial Office.

INTERNATIONAL ORGANIZATION PUBLICATIONS

GENERAL—*International Trade and Arrangements*

1. *International Cartels—A League of Nations Memorandum.* (Sales No. 1948 II.D.2)   New York 1947.   53 pp., $0.50   (D)

    An analysis of the reasons for the establishment of international cartels, their suitability for achieving their objectives; their effects on industrial structure and their economic implications. Three detailed appended tables provide valuable information about specific cartels of the inter-war period.

2. *International Tax Agreements.* (Sales No. 1948-52 XVI.1 to 6) New York 1948-52;   Pages and prices vary.   (A-c)

    A six volume listing of International Tax Agreements 1943-1951. The agreements are classified into nine categories; The following have relevance to underdeveloped areas:

    Vol. A.   *General Agreement on Income and Property Taxes.*

    Vol. C.   *Agreements on Taxation of Commercial or Industrial Enterprises.*

3. *List of Multilateral Conventions, Agreements, etc., Relating to Transport and Communications Questions.* (Sales No. 1948 VIII.1) New York 92 pp., $0.75.   (D)

    Lists conventions and international agreements of 34 countries with respect to transit, navigation. traffic, power, etc. There is no analytical discussion.

4. *Relative Prices of Exports and Imports of Underdeveloped Countries. A Study of Post-War Terms of Trade Between Underdeveloped and Industrialized Countries.* (Sales No. 1949. II.B.3)   Lake Success, 1949.   156 pp., $1.00   (A-a)   (D)

    Analyses of the prices of capital goods imported by underdeveloped countries relative to the prices of their exports. It also analyzes terms of trade for individual underdeveloped countries in relation to development.

5. *The Effects of Taxation on Foreign Trade and Investment.* (Sales No. 1950. XVI.1)   New York, 1950.   84 pp., $0.50   (A-c)

    A general study of the effects of taxes on foreign trade and investment from the viewpoint of both the capital exporting country and the underdeveloped areas receiving investments. The study is analytical, and examples are drawn from both developed and underdeveloped countries. Three annexes provide information on international agreements with respect to income and property taxes.

6. *Balance of Payment Trends and Policies 1950-51.* (Sales No. 1951. II.D.3) New York 1951. 50 pp., $0.40 (A-c)

   Based on a questionnaire submitted to member and non-member governments participating in regional commissions. It is analytical, and deals with policies and events in the fields of international trade and investment for 1950-51.

7. *Instability of Export Markets of Underdeveloped Countries.* (Sales No. 1952 II.A.1) New York 1952. 94 pp., $1.00. (A-a) (D)

   An analytical and statistical study dealing with the relations between exports of farm products by underdeveloped areas and the world prices of the commodities exported. Eighteen primary commodities are selected for analysis. Both short and long range fluctuations of prices are considered.

8. *A Study of Trade Between Asia and Europe.* (Sales No. 1953 II.F.3), Geneva 1953, 146 pp., $1.50 (D)

   Discusses the trade between Asia and Europe and between Asia and the rest of the world. Imports and exports of Asia including the Far East are analyzed.

   Commodity appendices discuss rubber, jute, tea, tin, rice, oil, cotton, and wool. Tables and charts are included.

9. *Economic Development of Underdeveloped Countries; Relative Prices of Primary Products and Manufactures in International Trade.* New York 1953, 107 pp., mimeographed—no price. (A-a)

   A technical study of the relative price movements of farm products, producer's goods, and consumer's goods from 1948 through the first half of 1952. Detailed breakdowns for individual commodities and closely related groups of commodities are given.

10. *Commodity Trade and Economic Development.* (Sales No. 1954 II.B.1), New York 1954, 102 pp., $0.75. (A-c) (D)

    A report prepared by a group of experts. They point out the great degree of mutual interest which exists in trade between the underdeveloped and the developed countries. It also analyzes national and international measures to be considered in dealing with the general problem of instability both from the monetary and the commodity viewpoint.

11. *Review of International Commodity Problems.* (Sales No. Year II.D Arabic No.) pages and prices vary. (A-a) (D)

    An Annual, first issued in 1948, replacing the *Review of International Commodity Arrangements* which was issued in 1947.

    The Annual Review analyzes the current situation of the principally internationally traded commodities. Commodity agreements, prices, supply and demand problems, intergovernmental action, etc., are discussed. Statistical tables, appendices and graphs are included.

GENERAL—*Technical Assistance and Economic Development*

12. *Technical Assistance for Economic Development.* (Sales No. 1948
    II.B.2) Lake Success, September 1948. 102 pp., $0.80 (A-b)   (D)
    A handbook of the resources of the United Nations and its specialized
    agencies which may assist nations in their programs of economic develop-
    ment.

13. *Technical Assistance for Economic Development. Plan for an Ex-
    panded Cooperative Program Through the United Nations and the
    Specialized Agencies.* (Sales No. 1949 II.B.1) New York 1949, 328
    pp. $2.50   (A-b)   (D)
    Part I analyzes the nature and the objectives of the technical assistance
    programs, the areas of interest and the proposed organizational and finan-
    cial arrangements.
    Part II considers the proposed policies of the several organizations:
    International Labor Organization, Food and Agriculture Organization,
    United Nations Educational and Scientific Organization, World Health
    Organization, International Trade Organization, International Monetary
    Fund, International Refugee Organization, International Bank for Recon-
    struction and Development, and International Civil Aviation Organization.
    The discussions are oriented towards specific programs. Cost estimates are
    given.

14. *Standards and Techniques of Public Administration—With Special
    Reference to Technical Assistance for Underdeveloped Areas.* (Sales
    No. 1951 II.B.7)   New York 1951, 65 pp., $0.50   (A-b)   (D)
    A useful guide to ways and means of securing technical assistance for
    underdeveloped countries from the United Nations and its Agencies. Dis-
    cussion also includes general principles, procedures of public administra-
    tion and measures for the improvement of such administration.

15. *Expanded Program of Technical Assistance. Fourth Report of the
    Technical Assistance Board to the Technical Assistance Committee.*
    New York May 8, 1952. Mimeographed—329 pp., No price. (A-b)
    (D)
    A detailed descriptive summary of technical assistance received by vari-
    ous countries and of the expanded program through the first financial
    period, July, 1950 to December 31, 1951. It includes technical assistance
    projects completed during the first financial period, those in operation at
    the end of the period, and projects which the participating organizations
    had agreed to initiate under agreements approved before December, 1951.

GENERAL—*Capital Formation and Economic Development*

16. *Economic Development in Selected Countries: Plans, Programs and
    Agencies.* a. Vol. 1 (Sales No. 1948 II.B.1), New York 1947. 286 pp.,
    $3.00 (A-b)   (D)

The following countries are included in Volume I: Anglo-Egyptian, Sudan, Argentina, Bolivia, Brazil, British African Non-Self-Governing and non-Metropolitan Territories, Chile, Egypt and other countries of the Middle East, French North Africa and French African Overseas Territories, India, Liberia, Mexico, Peru, Poland, Venezuela, and Yugoslavia.

b. Vol. II (Sales No. 1950 II.B.1), New York 1950. 271 pp., $2.00

Volume II deals with Australia, Bulgaria, Colombia, New Zealand, the Philippines, Puerto Rico, Southern Rhodesia, and the Union of South Africa.

(A-b)   (D)

Both reports offer a factual description of the more significant aspects of each country's program for economic development. There is included a brief survey of the governmental organizations responsible for the implementation of the program.

17. *Methods of Financing Economic Development in Underdeveloped Countries.* (Sales No. 1949 II.B.4) New York 1949, 163 pp., $1.25

(A-a)   (D)

A United Nations Secretariat report giving the views of the International Bank for Reconstruction and Development, the International Monetary Fund, the Food and Agriculture Organization, the International Labor Office, the International Chamber of Commerce and certain other United Nations Agencies on ways and means of financing economic development. It is a general analysis of domestic savings and investments, tax arrangements, foreign investments and other economic elements on capital accumulation.

18. *Domestic Financing of Economic Development.* (Sales No. 1951 II.B.1) New York 1950. 231 pp., $1.50 (A-a) (A-c) (A-b) (D)

This report is divided into two parts. The first part is a general discussion of savings and investment, with some incidental references to particular countries, some of which are underdeveloped.

The second part, an Annex, discusses prevailing practices and problems of domestic financing in Chile, Egypt, India, Mexico, Philippines, Puerto Rico, and United Kingdom Dependent Areas. It is analytical and historical rather than statistical.

19. *Economic Development of Underdeveloped Countries, Land Reform.* New York 1951, Mimeographed, 119 pp., No price. (A-b)

Describes the main features of agrarian structure in underdeveloped countries by means of example, and deals with the size and layout of farms, conditions of tenancy, agricultural credit, determination of legal title to land and water rights, communal tenure and the special problems presented by estates and plantations. There is also a discussion of the relations between the agrarian structure and economic development.

20. *Economic Development of Underdeveloped Countries. Volume and Distribution of National Income in Underdeveloped Countries.* New York June, 1951. Mimeographed—41 pp., No price. (A-a) (A-b) (D)

A statistical study of the estimated income and its distribution in various developed and underdeveloped countries. Most data are for 1948 and 1949. Data on earnings and income of agricultural and non-agricultural groups are available; proportionate distributions of incomes given where available.

21. *Report of the Working Party of Experts on Mobilization of Domestic Capital.* Bangkok, 1951. Mimeographed, 47 pp., no price. (A-c) (A-b)   (D)

A general discussion of problems faced in the mobilization of indigenous capital for economic development. Appendix 3 contains a bibliography of 34 reports on mobilization of domestic capital.

22. *Measures for the Economic Development of the Underdeveloped Countries.* (Sales No. 1951 II.B.2) New York 1951. 108 pp., $0.75 (A-b)   (A-c)

A monograph on economic development prepared by a group of international experts. It is not concerned with underdevelopment problems in any particular country, but rather is a general treatise on underdevelopment and growth. It suggests alternative programs of action, including programs of international trade and external capital acquisition.

23. a. *Mobilization of Domestic Capital: Report and Documents of the First Working Party of Experts.* (Sales No. 1953 II.F.2) Bangkok, 1952. 206 pp., $1.50 (A-c)   (D) ; b. *Mobilization of Domestic Capital: Report and Documents of the Second Working Party.* Bangkok, 1953. 334 pp., $2.50 (A-c)   (D)

The first report consists of a series of papers dealing with various aspects of Far Eastern inflation, with recommendations as to its control. The papers deal with three major topics: inflation: measures for increasing government bond sales; and measures for mobilizing savings.

The orientation of the second report is toward problems of foreign and domestic capital mobilization. Technical papers dealing with; measures for encouraging capital mobilization, industrial and agricultural finance, development corporations for Asia and the Far East, and the relations between foreign and domestic capital mobilization, are included.

The technical papers of both volumes are analytical, often with suggestive recommendations. Statistical data are presented to support particular arguments.

26. *The International Flow of Private Capital 1946-1952.* (Sales No. 1954. II.D.1) New York 1954, 61 pp., $0.40 (A-a-b-c)   (C)

A study divided into three parts. The first analyzes the general trend of investment, compares it with that of the 1920's and offers a global measure of investment. Investments of the United States, the United Kingdom, Switzerland, France, Belgium and Canada are discussed.

The second part discusses the tendencies of investment practice.

The third part discusses factors limiting the flow of capital. National and international factors are discussed.

Tables are included.

27. *Special Study on Economic Conditions and Development in Non-Self-Governing Territories.* (Sales No. Year VI.B.1) Annual. New York. Prices and pages vary. (A-b) (D)

An annual presenting a detailed factual and statistical report on economic and social conditions in non-self-governing areas. The reports are detailed and cover such varied aspects as; agriculture, industry, fisheries, finance, foreign trade, demography, health, welfare, education, fiscal matters, etc. The basic material for these reports is submitted annually to the Secretary General by the Administering Government. Prior to 1952, the reports were arranged according to the submitting governments, subsequent to 1952 the arrangement is by geographical area.

GENERAL—*Miscellaneous*

28. *Housing and Town and Country Planning.* Bulletin No. 1 (Sales No. 1948 IV.7) New York 1948. 57 pp., $1.50 (B-1) (D)

The first part contains essays on town and country planning, village planning in India, and other technical matters. The second part report is an extensive and useful bibliography of books and pamphlets on planning (social and economic, regional and national, town and country).

29. *Catalogue of Economic and Social Projects of the United Nations and the Specialized Agencies.* (Sales No. Year II.D.1ff) Pages and prices vary. New York 1949 ff. (D)

An annual catalogue of works planned or completed by the United Nations and the Specialized Agencies. (The Catalogue was preceded by one titled *The Directory of Economic and Statistical Projects. No. 1, Series 1,* issued 1948, representing the same coverage as the Catalogue.) When considered appropriate, supplements to the Catalogue are issued.

The *Catalogue* is an invaluable descriptive index of the work of the Secretariat of the United Nations, and of the Specialized Agencies in the economic and social fields. Included in the Catalogue are titles and descriptive studies and surveys, as well as technical services and operational activities of the various United Nations Specialized Agencies with respect to social and economic matters.

In addition to describing work already accomplished, and published, the *Catalogue* indicates work in process and work projected.

30. *An International Index of Films on the Conservation and Utilization of Resources.* (Sales No. 1950, II.B.10) Mimeographed. Prepared by UNESCO 1949. New York 1950. 175 pp., $1.00 (D)

An index of films dealing with conservation and utilization of resources. The information for each film includes the title, the length in minutes, the organization which produced or distributes the film, date of production, country of origin and a short description of the content. Size of the film is also given. The subjects of the films include conservation of resources, mineral resources, fuels and underground water, forest land resources, wild life and marine resources, etc.

31. *World Iron Ore Resources and Their Utilization.* (Sales No. 1950, II.D.3) New York 1950. 74 pp., $0.80. (A-a)   (D)

    Brings together world-wide data on iron ore resources and such related factors as availability of coking coal. It analyzes the economic development involved in utilizing resources. The iron ore resources of underdeveloped areas are discussed in some detail.

32. *Proceedings of the United Nations Scientific Conference on the Conservation and Utilization of Resources.* (Sales No. 1950 II.B.2-8) V.1 *Plenary Meetings,* 431 pp., $4.50; V.2 *Mineral Resources,* 257 pp., $3.00; V.3 *Fuel and Energy Resources,* 333 pp., $3.00; V.4 *Water Resources* 466 pp., $4.50; V.5 *Forest Resources,* 325 pp., $3.00; V.6 *Land Resources,* 629 pp., $6.00; V.7 *Wild Life, and Fish Resources,* 250 pp., $2.50; New York 1950. (A-a)   (D)

    These seven volumes deal with scientific papers and discussions on resources (see volume titles). The papers do not deal specifically with underdeveloped areas, but frequent references are made to resource availabilities in underdeveloped areas.

33. *Land Reform—Defects in Agrarian Structure as Obstacles to Economic Development.* (Sales No. 1951 II.B.3) New York 1951. 101 pp., $0.75 (A-b)

    Analyzes farm holdings, size, water rights, etc., in underdeveloped areas and offers suggested types of reforms. While the study is general in scope, specific case-examples are given.

34. *Preliminary Report on the World Social Situation, with Special Reference to Standards of Living.* (Sales No. 1952 IV.II) New York 1952. 180 pp., $1.75. (A-a)   (B-4)   (D)

    A broad survey of the amenities of life, standards of living, schooling and general social conditions of the entire World. The study is highly instructive because of the comparative nature of the data.

35. *Special Study on Social Conditions in Non-Self-Governing Territories.* (Sales No. 1953. VI.B.2) New York 1953, 270 pp., $2.00 (A) (B)

    A survey of social conditions in the non-self-governing territories. Such social problems as race relations, public health, standards of living, welfare and international cooperation are considered. The data are presented for each particular non-self-governing territory. The orientation is factual and statistical.

36. *Rural Progress Through Co-operatives.* (Sales No. 1954. II.B.2) New York, 1954, 112 pp., $0.75. (A-b)   (D)

    Discusses the different tasks which must be effectively accomplished if agriculture is to succeed. Then it considers in detail how far co-operative societies can perform these tasks in different sets of natural, social and

economic circumstances. An appendix covering the activities of the ILO
and the FAO in the field of co-operatives is also included.

37. *Progress in Land Reform.* (Sales No. 1954 II.B.3), New York 1954,
   322 pp., $2.50 (A-b)
   A joint report of the United Nations, the Food and Agriculture Organization, and the International Labor Organizations.
   It discusses land ownership and land reform of the various countries of
   the world. Appendices, indexes and statistical tables are included.

STATISTICAL

38. *Transport and Communications Review.* Annual subscription $2.00,
   single copy $0.50. (A-b)   (D)
   A quarterly report consisting of unrelated technical studies of various
   phases of transportation. Occasional articles on underdeveloped countries
   appear e.g. *Transportation Problems in Southern Africa* (Volume 6 No. 2
   April-June 1953), the *State of Transport and Communications in Turkey*
   (Volume 6 No. 1 January-March 1953.)

39. a. *Economic Report. Salient Features of the World Economic Situation 1945-1947.* (Sales No. 1948 II.C.1) New York 1948, 354 pp.,
   $2.50 (Entire outline).
   b. *Supplement to Economic Report, Salient Features of the World
   Economic Situation,* 1945-1947. (Sales No. 1948 II.C.2) New York
   1948, 140 pp., $1.00 (Entire outline).

40. *World Economic Report*—Annual (Sales No. Year II.C. Arabic No.)
   Pages and prices vary. (Entire outline).
   A statistical and analytical resume of the Year's economic development
   in production, distribution, international trade and payments, employment, etc. The *Report* is world wide in scope, specific data being presented
   for various countries. Annual comparisons are made, and the economic
   history of the previous year is analyzed.
   The first Annual Supplement of the *World Economic Report* is for
   1949-50. Supplements concerned with Africa and the Middle East have
   appeared since 1951. These supplements complement the regional surveys
   prepared for Europe, Asia, the Far East and for Latin America. The Supplements appear periodically usually on an annual basis.

41. *Review of Economic Conditions in Africa. Supplement to World
   Economic Report.* (Year) Sales No. Year II.C. Arabic No.) New
   York. Pages and prices vary. (Entire outline).

42. *Final Report of the United Nations Economic Survey Mission for
   the Middle East.* (Sales No. 1949 II.B.5) (Part I) New York 1949,

103 pp., $1.00 (Sales No. 1949 II.B.5) (Part II) New York 1949, 74 pp., $0.80 (Entire outline).

The orientation of the report is toward recommendations concerning the Arab refugee problem. The refugee problem, however, is "inseparable from the problem of poverty and hunger (of) a large section of the population of the Middle East". The report, therefore, is a general set of recommendations for development, supported by a short economic and social analysis. (See Title 83).

Part II, the *Technical Supplement,* examines some of the agricultural and engineering problems and projects.

43. *Review of Economic Conditions in the Middle East.* (Year). *Supplement to World Economic Report.* (Sales No. year II.C. Arabic No.) New York. Pages and prices vary. (Entire outline).

These supplements present more detailed data than those that are available in the *World Economic Report.* Data are presented for smaller geographical and political units than in the *World Economic Report.*

44. *Recent Changes in Production, Supplement to World Economic Report,* 1950-51 (Sales No. 1952. II.C.1) New York 1952. 120 pp., $1.00. (Entire outline).

Complements the analysis of major national economic changes and changes in international trade and payments presented in the *World Economic Report, 1950-51.*

45. *Economic Survey of Latin America.* (Sales No. Year. II.G. Arabic No.) Annual. First issue 1948. Pages and prices vary (Entire outline). (Argentina, Bolivia, Brazil, Chile, Colombia, Costa Rica, **Cuba, Dominican Republic, Ecuador, El Salvador, Guatemala, Haiti, Honduras, Mexico, Nicaragua, Panama, Paraguay, Peru, Uruguay, Venezuela.)**

46. *Economic Survey of Asia and the Far East.* (Sales No. Year. II.F. Arabic No.). Annual, First issue 1949. New York. Pages and prices vary. (Entire outline.) (Associated States of Indo-China.) (Cam-**bodia, Laos and Vietnam, British Borneo Territories, Burma, Cey-lon, China, Hongkong, India, Indonesia, Korea, the Federation of Malaya, Singapore, Nepal, Pakistan, the Philippines, Thailand and Japan.)**

Annual surveys in even greater detail than the Supplements to the *World Economic Report.* They are invaluable sources of economic data and analysis; such matters as resources, income generation and distribution, economic development, agricultural and industrial production, transport, international trade, international payments, money, credit, finance, manpower are all treated both generally and in many instances specifically for particular countries involved.

47. *Demographic Yearbook.* (Sales No. Year. XIII. Arabic No.) New York. Pages and prices vary. (A-a)

First issued in 1948 by the Statistical Office of the United Nations. This yearbook is a comprehensive collection of international demographic statistics. Most of the countries and areas of the world are included.

48. *Statistical Yearbook.* (Sales No. Year. XVII. Arabic No.) New York. Pages and prices vary. (D)

First issued in 1948 by the Statistical Office of the United Nations. Contains statistical data of many economic, trade, demographic, etc., aspects for over two hundred countries and areas. Data to 1928 are often presented. An appendix and an index are included.

49. *Yearbook of International Trade Statistics.* (Year). (Sales No. Year XVII Arabic No.) New York. Pages and prices vary. (A-c)

The *Yearbook of International Trade Statistics,* prepared by the Statistical Office of the United Nations, Department of Economic Affairs. (First published in 1951 for 1950.) Quantities and values of goods in international trade by country of origin and country of destination are presented in this annual. The *Yearbook* for 1950 gives 1938 data when available, and in some instances earlier data, so that comparisons may be made between post-war and pre-war years. No analysis of the statistical data is offered.

Data on principal commodities are presented. This *Yearbook* is a continuation of *International Trade Statistics,* published by the League of Nations for the years 1933-1939.

50. *Population Bulletin.* (Sales No. Year XIII Arabic No.) Pages and prices vary. (A-a)

First issued as an occasional series in December, 1951. A statistical and analytical report on demography. The Bulletin does not contain continuous series but rather discreet monographic reports. Some materials on underdeveloped areas are included.

51. *Population Studies.* (Sales No. Year Arabic No.) Prices and pages vary. (A-a)

No. 1 *Population of Western Samoa.* No. 2 and 14. *Population of Tanganyika.* No. 5 *Problems of Migration Statistics.* No. 7 *Methods of Using Census Statistics for Calculation of Life Table and Other Demographic Measures With Special Reference to Brazil.* These reports are an analysis of migration and demographic statistics and their collection. The technical reports in this series e.g. fertility data and population censuses and methods of using census statistics are of value in compiling and analyzing statistics on population.

52. *Monthly Bulletin of Statistics.* Annual subscription $5.00, single copies $0.50. Pages vary.

A monthly statistical report of economic and social life of United Nations and non-member countries. Series present available information on:

population and vital statistics, employment and unemployment, industrial production, fuel and man-power, raw materials, manufacturers, food, internal and external trade, transport, finance, wages and prices. The data represent probably the most authoritative set of comparative international data presently available. *The Monthly Bulletin* is most useful for current and comparative figures on virtually all phases of economic and social life. These reports indicate that, at best, the statistics for many underdeveloped areas are fragmentary.

53. *Public Finance Information Papers.* Peru. (Sales No. 1952. XVI.2) New York, 62 pp., $0.50; Iraq (Sales No. 1951. XVI.6) New York, 43 pp., $0.25; Egypt (Sales No. 1951. XVI.7) Lake Success, 31 pp., $0.15; Colombia (Sales No. 1951. XVI.8) Lake Success, 41 pp., $0.20; Italy (Sales No. 1951. XVI.9) Lake Success, 80 pp., $0.40; Iran (Sales No. 1951. XVI.4) New York, 102 pp., $0.50. (A-c)

This series stems from the preliminary report: *Public Finance Data* (document 31 E/CN.8/ and annexes), published during 1948/49, which covered the following countries; Argentina, Austria, Belgium, Brazil, Canada, Chile, China, Costa Rica, Guatemala, India, Iran, Ireland, Japan, Mexico, New Zealand, Norway, Portugal, Sweden, Switzerland, United Kingdom, United States, USSR, and Venezuela. These papers provide a background of the development of public finance and an analysis of the current situation. Expenditures, receipts, finances, budgetary systems and statistical appendix make up the detail of report. Special consideration is given to certain economic development programs.

54. *Public Finance Surveys.* (India) (Sales No. 1952. XVI.2) New York, 101 pp., $0.75. Venezuela (Sales No. 1951. XVI.2) New York, 87 pp., $0.75. (A-c)

Case Studies of selected underdeveloped countries whose public finance systems present problems which are likely to be of broad interest and applicability. The *Surveys* are broader in scope and more analytical than the *Information Papers.* Reports on Venezuela and India have been published, others are in preparation.

55. *Statistical Papers*

Series A—*Population and Vital Statistics Reports.* (Quarterly) $0.25 per issue. (Sales No. Year. XII. Arabic No.) New York. (A-a)

Series B—*Statistical Notes (Current Events in International Statistics).*—Periodically. (D)

Series C—*Sample Surveys of Current Interest.* (Periodical Reports) (Sales No. Year. XVII. Arabic No.) New York. (A-c)

The purpose of this series is to assist those interested in the application of modern sampling techniques by making available, in summary form, the experiences gained by various statisticians and statistical organizations in the field.

Series D—*Commodity Trade Statistics.* Quarterly—New York. Price per copy $1.00. Annual subscription $4.00. (A-a)

Value of import and export trade, in United States dollars and metric units, for 150 commodity groups is presented.

Series E—*National and Per Capita Incomes, Income Distribution, etc.* (Periodically) (Sales No. Year. XVII. Arabic No.) New York. Pages and prices vary. (Series E is published under different numbers according to material dealt with).

A comparative study of national income and per capita income for selected countries, some developed, some underdeveloped. The report shows the unevenness of statistics in various countries included in the survey. Some interesting estimates of investment and productivity are included. The reports are analytical as well as statistical.

Series F—*Studies in Methods.* No. 1, *Index Numbers of Industrial Production,* 1950. $0.25. (D)

Covers aims and uses of index numbers, relationship to other general economic indicators and to national income accounting, etc.

Series H—*Statistics of National Incomes and Expenditures.* (Sales No. Year. XVII. Arabic No.) New York. (Semi-Annual) $0.50 (A-a)

A statistical presentation of a simplified national product and distribution accounting for selected developed and underdeveloped countries. Sources of the data are given so the report is a useful bibliography of statistical series.

Series M: (D)

No.   1: *Nomenclature of Geographic Areas for Statistical Purposes,* New York 1949.

No.   2: *Report on the First Latin American Training Centre on Statistics and Censuses, Mexico, 1948,* New York 1949.

No.   3: *Indexes of Quantum in International Trade,* New York 1949.

No.   4: *International Standard Industrial Classification of All Economic Activities.* New York. (undated).

No.   5: *Report on the European Centre of Applied Agricultural and Demographic Statistics, Paris, 1949,* New York, 1949.

No.   6: *Report on the International Training Centres on Statistics and Censuses for the Near East Countries,* Cairo, 1949.

No.   7: *Report on the International Training Centres on Statistics and Censuses for South East Asia and Oceania,* New Delhi, 1949-50.

No.   8: *International Standard Definitions for Transport Statistics,* New York 1950.

No. 9: *Report on the Inter-American Seminar for Biostatistics,* Santiago, 1950.

No. 10: *Standard International Trade Classification,* New York 1951, $1.50

No. 11: *List of Statistical Series Collected by International Organizations,* New York.

No. 12: *Report on International Training on Vital Statistics and Health. Statistics for South East Asia,* New York.

No. 13: *Report on the Training Center on Vital Statistics and Health Statistics for the Eastern Mediterranean.* New York.

No. 14: *Retail Prices Comparisons for International Salary Determination.* New York. (1952) $0.40.

No. 15: *Report on the Western Pacific Regional Seminar on Vital Statistics and Health Statistics.* New York.

No. 16: *Report and Proceedings of the United Nations International Seminar on Statistical Organization. Ottawa, 13 October-6 November,* New York 1953. $1.50

No. 17: *International Standards in Basic Industrial Statistics,* New York 1953, $0.30.

No. 19: *Principles for a Vital Statistics System.* New York 1953. $0.30.

Series T.

Direction of International Trade. New York Annual subscription $5.00, $0.50 per copy. (A-c)

Joint publication of the United Nations, the International Monetary Fund and the International Bank for Reconstruction and Development, giving monthly figures for trade origin, and destination. Data presented in United States dollars.

REGIONAL—*Africa*

56. *A General Economic Appraisal of Libya.* (Sales No. 1952. II.H.2) New York 1952. 56 pp., $0.60 (A-a) (A-b) (B-1)

The first part briefly discusses the land, people and their social background. The next section, dealing with the economic conditions is the major part of the report; it deals with the institutional and the source background of the country. The last part deals with economic policy and conditions of development. The recommendations are fairly general.

57. *The Trust Territory of Somaliland under Italian Administration.* (Sales No. 1953. II.H.2) New York 1952. Mimeographed. 348 pp., $3.50 (A-a) (A-b) (D)

Prepared for the Government of Italy by an expert appointed by the United Nations Technical Assistance Administration and by experts appointed respectively by the Food and Agriculture Organization, the United Nations Educational and Scientific Organization, and the World Health Organization.

It examines the agricultural, industrial, foreign trade and resource potential in Somaliland and makes recommendations for the development of that country. School systems are also discussed. The orientation of this study is along developmental lines rather than toward the history and present situation of the country.

58. *World Economic Situation. Aspects of Economic Development in Africa.* Report by the Secretary General. New York, 1953. Mimeographed. 171 pp., No price. (A-a) (D)

Deals with the production, and exchange of commodities produced in Africa. The major orientation is toward agricultural products. There is a discussion of the commercialization of agriculture in Africa and its attendant effects on employment, capital and subsistence agriculture.

59. *The Economic and Social Development of Libya.* (Sales No. 1953. II.H.8), New York 1953, 170 pp., $1.75. (A) (B) (D)

Prepared by the Technical Assistance Administration of the United Nations. Financial considerations, and the principles and problems of economic development are discussed, as are education, industry, commerce, public utilities, transport, labor problems and labor policies, and social security.

60. *Enlargement of the Exchange Economy in Tropical Africa.* (Sales No. 1954, II.C.4), New York 1954, 59 pp., $0.40. (A, b, c) (D)

Deals with the structural changes taking place in the economics of tropical Africa as a result of an increase in production for market. It throws light on the economic condition of the non-white communities.

REGIONAL—*Asia and the Far East*

61. *Economic Bulletin for Asia and the Far East.* Issued three times a year. (Prepared by the Research and Statistics Division, Economic Mission for Asia and the Far East). Volume 1, No. 1 issued August 1950. Bangkok. Pages vary, $0.50 per issue.

Provides a regular review of the economic situation in Asia and the Far East for the interval between publications of the *Annual Survey*. Reports consist of a review of the economic situation in Asia and the Far East; followed by a series of notes on varied economic matters. The third and last section consists of Asian economic statistics and is a valuable compilation of data dealing with production, trade, and prices. These are continuing series.

62. *Formulation and Economic Appraisal of Development Projects.* Lahore, Pakistan, 1950. Vol. 1 (Sales No. 1951. II.B.4. Vol. 1) 473 pp., $3.00. Vol. II (Sales No. 1951. II.B.4 Vol. II), 474-780 pp., $2.50 (A-b)

   A series of lectures by experts delivered at the Asian Center on Agriculture and Allied Projects in Lahore, Pakistan, during the Fall of 1950. The first volume is largely devoted to general lectures on basic principles of development. The orientation is economic, financial and administrative. The second volume is primarily concerned with lectures on specific technical subjects related to economic development. While the whole book represents a very high level of competence, the problems discussed vary in nature from discussions of economic theories to consideration of multipurpose river projects.

63. *Fields of Economic Development Handicapped by Lack of Trained Personnel in Certain Countries of Asia and the Far East.* (Sales No. 1951. II.F.6) Bangkok, 1951. 119 pp., $0.75. (A-b) (C-3)

   Discusses the need of skilled foreign and indigenous personnel in industrial and public utilities' undertakings for Burma, Ceylon, India, Cambodia, Laos and Vietnam, Indonesia, Korea, Nepal, Pakistan, Philippines, Thailand and United Kingdom Territories. Technical personnel needs in major industries are outlined, and suggestions of ways to satisfy the lack of personnel are given.

64. *Foreign Investment Laws and Regulations of Countries of Asia and the Far East.* (Sales No. 1951. II.F.1) New York 1951. 88 pp., $0.75. (A-c)

   A handbook of governmental policies and legal regulations regarding investment for Burma, Ceylon, India, Hongkong, Indo China, Indonesia, Japan, Pakistan, Philippines, Singapore, Malaya, and Thailand.

65. *Mobilization of Domestic Capital in Certain Countries of Asia and The Far East* (Sales No. 1951. II.F.3) Bangkok 1951. 239 pp., $1.50. (A-a) (A-b) (D)

   The first five chapters deal with the economic resources and institutions of Asiatic and Far Eastern countries, with discussions of production, capital and money markets, and the role of government. The second section analyzes the monetary, fiscal and banking institutions of Burma, Ceylon, India, Indonesia, Pakistan, the Philippines, and Thailand.

66. *Flood Control Series:*
   Flood Damage and Flood Control Activities in Asia and the Far East, Methods and Problems of Flood Control in Asia and the Far East. (Proceedings of the regional technical conference on flood control in Asia and the Far East). Flood Control series.

   a. No. 1 (Sales No. 1951 II.F.2) Bangkok 1950, 81 pp., and maps. $1.50. (A-a) (A-b) (D)

A study of the hydrology and meteorology of Asia and the Far East. The analysis is supported by statistical tables and maps. Flood damage and proposed techniques for flood control are included in the discussion. The orientation of the major part of the survey is directed toward the major rivers of Asia and the Far East.

b. No. 2, (1951 II.F.5) Bangkok 1951. 45 pp., additional plates. (A-b) (D)

Concerned essentially with the review of flood control methods used in the various countries of the Far East. It is a technical report with no specific geographic orientation.

c. No. 3 (Sales No. 1953 II.F.1) Bangkok 1952. 320 pp., including graphs and plates. $3.00 (A-b) (D)

Divided into two parts; the first, *Proceedings,* consists of a brief report on discussions regarding flood control. This part comprehends the first 33 pages of the report. The second part consists of technical papers on various aspects of flood control and on specific experiences in technique utilized in particular instances.

d. No. 4 *River Training and Bank Protection.* (Sales No. 1953. II.F.6) Bangkok, 1953. 100 pp., $0.80. (D)

This is the fourth in the Flood Control Series. It discusses the various methods of river training and deals with river training works in Asia and the Far East. This study analyzes different methods of bank protection. It compares works in the region with those outside. The study concludes with recommendations. Pertinent illustrations are included.

e. No. 5. *The Sediment Problem.* (Sales No. 1953. II.F.7), Bangkok 1953, 92 pp., $0.80. (D)

This is the fifth in the Flood Control Series. It discusses briefly the extent of soil erosion in the area (Asia and the Far East). It analyzes fully the sediment problem after the soil enters natural streams or canals. The study concerns transportation of sediment, silting of canals and reservoirs, and the action of sediment on the rivers. It is highly technical. Illustrations, graphs and tables are included.

67. *The National Income of the Philippines and its Distribution.* (Sales No. 1953, II.H.3) Mimeo.—New York 1952. 44 pp., $0.40. (A-a)

National income data for the years 1946-1951 are presented. There are also data regarding agricultural crops by type, and income generation by specific Philippine districts.

68. *Coal and Iron Ore Resources of Asia and the Far East.* (Sales No. 1952. II.F.1) Bangkok 1952, 155 pp., $1.50. (A-a) (D)

The first part deals with the Far East generally, and discusses coal and iron resources. This comprises 32 pages of the entire report. The second part consists of chapters on the countries of the Far East where coal and iron ore exist. Detailed information about mining methods are given by district. It is illustrated by plates and maps.

69. *Report of the Mission on Community-Organization and Development in South and Southeast Asia.* (Sales No. 1953. IV.24), New York 1953, mimeographed, 167 pp., $2.50.

    Prepared for the Technical Assistance Administration of the United Nations dealing with India, Ceylon, Thailand and the Philippines. The report analyzes national community programs and voluntary agencies concerned with training and technical assistance. Specific recommendations are given. Such aspects as education, economics and training are included.

70. *Development of Mineral Resources in Asia and the Far East.* (Sales No. 1953, II.F.5) Bangkok 1953. 366 pp., $3.50. (D)

    Part I discusses the development of mineral resources in the region and possibilities of increasing production. National and international activities in the field of mineral resources development are analyzed. Recommendations are given. Part II deals with technical material such as, geological surveys of fuel, iron ore and non-ferrous metals. Resources of ferro-alloy metals are considered. The discussion is carried on a country by country basis. Statistical tables are included.

71. *Report of the Mission on Community Organization and Development in South and Southeast Asia.* (Sales No. 1953. IV.24) New York 1953, 167 pp., $2.50. (D)

    Prepared by the Technical Assistance Administration of the United Nations. It discusses and appraises the economic and social aspects of national community programs. The role of voluntary agencies, training and technical assistance are also discussed. Particular projects from India, Ceylon, Thailand and the Philippines are also discussed. Recommendations are made.

REGIONAL—*Latin America*

72. *Mission to Haiti.* (Sales No. 1949. II.B.2) New York 1949. 327 pp., $2.50 (A-a) (D)

    A comprehensive, economic, demographic and social analysis of Haitian society. Various measures are proposed to increase the efficiency of the national development and to hasten its pace. No cost estimates for the suggested programs are given, but some fiscal suggestions are offered.

73. *Agricultural Requisites in Latin America.* (Sales No. 1950 II.G.1) New York 1950. 156 pp., $1.25. (A-b)

    A report on the technical needs of Latin American agriculture and fisheries. A statistical appendix is largely devoted to United States exports of farm equipment to Latin America starting with 1938.

74. *The Economic Development of Latin America and its Principal Problems.* (Sales No. 1950, II.G.2) New York, 1950, 59 pp., $0.40 (A-b)

An attempt to explain the economic development of Latin America by the use of other concepts than those of traditional economics and historical analysis. The author develops a theory of peripheral economic development for areas such as Latin America.

75. *Report of the United Nations Economic Mission to Chile 1949-50.* (Sales No. 1951. II.B.6) New York 1951. 38 pp., $0.40. (A-a) (A-c) (D)

   The first part deals with short run problems of Chile, and is primarily concerned with inflation and the shortage of consumer goods. The second part deals with long-run problems, and is concerned with administrative, budgetary and tax and fiscal reforms. Detailed recommendations are offered. It is analytical rather than statistical.

76. *Labor Productivity of the Cotton Textile Industry in Five Latin American Countries.* (Sales No. 1951. II.G.2) New York 1951, 293 pp., $3.00 (A-a) (D)

   A detailed statistical and technical analysis of the productivity of textile labor in Brazil, Ecuador, Mexico, Peru and Chile.

77. *United States Income Taxation of Private United States Investments in Latin America.* (Sales No. 1953 XVI.1) New York 1953. 80 pp., $0.75. (A)

   Considers United States tax provisions and proposals which modify the tax obligations of the United States investors abroad, particularly in Latin America.

78. *A Study of Trade Between Latin America and Europe.* (Sales No. 1952. II.G.2) Geneva 1953. 117 pp., $1.25. (A-a) (D)

   A statistical and analytical study of foreign trade between particular countries in Latin America and particular countries in Europe. It also deals with trade in particular commodities. There are analytical appendices dealing with coffee, sugar, cotton, linseed and linseed oil, wool, meat, textile machinery and tractors. The analysis is presented in great statistical detail.

79. *Study on Iron and Steel Industry and Report on Meeting of Experts held in Bogota and Sponsored by ECLA and TAA.* Santiago. February 1953. Vol. I. 163 pp., Vol. II (Each section separately paged). Mimeographed. No price. (A-a) (D)

   A detailed statistical analysis of iron and steel in Latin America. Sources of iron and steel are discussed, domestic and foreign costs, the relation of cost to size and type of plants and other technical problems are considered. A list of Latin American experts participating in the meeting is given, with their addresses.

   Addendum I consists of five reports. The first is an analysis of the factors influencing iron and steel consumption in Latin America. It is a statistical report on a country by country basis.

Addendum II deals with the influence of local factors on the iron and steel industry in Latin America. This, too, is a statistical analysis on a country basis. Hypothetical plants are assumed in various areas of Latin America and their costs estimated.

Addendum III is concerned with the influence and the size of the market on the iron and steel industry in Latin America. The study is primarily devoted to the comparative cost analysis of hypothetical and real plants of varying size, furnishing markets of varying size.

Addendum IV is concerned with the structure of the steel fabricating industry in Latin America. The orientation of this study is the analysis of the economic relations between steel-using industries and basic steel, for the various countries of Latin America.

Addendum V is an outline of steel industries from Latin American Countries. Location and capacity of plants are discussed, and availability of ores and other raw materials are considered.

80. *Preliminary Study of the Technique of Programming Economic Development.* Santiago, 1953. 385 pp., Mimeographed, no price. (A-b) (D)

An analytical study using as examples Latin American data concerned with the integration of programming techniques. It goes into great detail showing the relationship between agriculture, foreign trade, consumption, industrial investment, etc. A hypothetical program for Chile is developed and analyzed.

81. *Problems of Intra-Regional Trade and Possibilities of Expanding Trade Among the South American Countries* (Argentina, Bolivia, Brazil, Chile, Paraguay, Peru and Uruguay). Rio de Janeiro, 1953. Vol. I, 126 pp., Vol. II, 123 pp., Mimeographed, no price. (A-a) (D)

Part I examines the structure of Latin American inter-regional trade, and considers the barriers to that trade. Price, financial, tariff, and other elements are included in the discussion of the structure of trade. Part II concentrates upon specific food stuffs and the industrial raw materials which are, or could be, traded between the countries of Latin America. Also discussed are production and consumption prospects, and problems arising out of the need to dispose of surpluses.

82. *Possibilities for the Development of the Pulp and Paper Industry in Latin America.* (Sales No. 1953. II.G.2) New York 1954, 142 pp., $1.50 (A-b) (D)

Joint study by the Economic Commission for Latin America and the Food and Agriculture Organization. Productive capacity supplies, and consumption of paper in Latin American countries are discussed. Statistical information about production, imports, exports, and consumption of paper are given.

Tables dealing with individual countries are included.

REGIONAL—*The Middle East*

83. *Final Report of the U.N. Economic Survey Mission for the Middle East* a. (Sales No. 1949. II.B.5) New York 103 pp., $1.80. Part I, the *Final Report and Appendices*, $1.00. b. Part II, the *Technical Supplement* (Sales No. 1949. II.B.5 Part II) New York 1949, 74 pp., $0.80. (A-a) (A-c) (D)

     (Saudi Arabia, Kuwait, Oman, the Hadhramaut, Aden and Yemen, Lebanon, Syria, Iraq, Jordan, and Israel).

     Prepared for the purpose of examining "the economic situation in the countries affected by the recent hostilities" between Israel and the Arab World. The official orientation therefore dealt largely with the Arab refugee problem. However, it was recognized that the "obstacles in the way of economic development in the Middle East are much the same as those hampering the rehabilitation of the Arab refugees", therefore the report is largely directed towards suggesting ways and means to further economic development in the Middle East.

     It examines the economic structure and resources of the Middle East, and to a lesser extent the social organization in that area. Recommendations of a rather general sort are made although Part II, the *Technical Supplement,* contains some specific agricultural and engineering data on particular sections of the countries involved.

84. *United Nations Social Welfare Seminar for Arab States in the Middle East.* Beirut, 15 August-8 September 1949 (Sales No. 1950. IV.8) New York 1950. 68 pp., $0.50 (B)

     Consists, first, of an outline of recommendations with respect to social welfare defined very broadly. The second part deals with an outline of the various lectures and seminar meetings. The welfare recommendations deal with those applicable to the Arab society of the Middle East and deal particularly with nomadic peoples, their welfare needs and methods for satisfying these needs. Legislation, family structure, economic organization, problems of delinquent and handicapped children, selection of students and other problems are considered.

85. *Second United Nations Social Welfare Seminar for Arab States in the Middle East.* Cairo 22 November-14 December 1950. (Sales No. 1951. IV.3) New York 1951. 87 pp., $0.50. (D)

     The Second Technical Assistance Administration Conference was held at Cairo in 1950. The orientation of this meeting was towards trade, employment, and production, rather than welfare. Such matters as village planning, education and rural welfare were considered.

86. *Revenue, Administration and Policy in Israel.* (Sales No. 1953. II.H.5) New York, 1953. 107 pp., $1.00. (A-c) (Prepared for the government of Israel by an expert appointed by the Technical Assistance Administration of the United Nations.)

It analyzes the revenue policy and structure of Israel and offers suggestions for change. Tax rates and arrangements are discussed and analyzed,
and alternative policy considerations are offered to the Government. In
addition to technical suggestions with respect to taxes, the report also
offers a suggestion for the training of officials.

87. *Report of the Mission on Community-Organization and Develop-
    ment in Selected Arab Countries of the Middle East.* (Sales No.
    1953, IV.21) Mimeographed. New York, 1953. 60 pp., $0.60. (B-3)

    Prepared by a United Nations mission. Included in the survey are
    Lebanon, Egypt, Iraq and Syria. The purpose of the mission was to pre-
    pare a report on community welfare and development in the above coun-
    tries. To this end, specific programs and projects were analyzed and
    recommendations offered. The major orientation is the village community.

88. *Report on Training of the Civil Service of Israel.* (Sales No. 1953
    II.H.7), Mimeographed, New York, 1953. 36 pp., $0.30. (C-3)

    Prepared by the United Nations technical assistance mission for the
    government of Israel. It is concerned with both educational and in-training
    needs and devices.

FOOD AND AGRICULTURE ORGANIZATION—*General and Statistical Studies.*

89. *World Food Survey*—Rome 1946. 39 pp., no price. (A-a) (A-b)
    (D)

    This report (the first) is an analysis of the caloric intake per capita of
    some seventy countries of the world, comprising about 90% of the world's
    population. The caloric intake and type of food consumed is compared to
    reasonable targets. Some general ideas of increasing food production are
    offered. (See Title 83).

90. *Second World Food Survey.* Rome 1952. 59 pp., $0.50 (A-a) (A-b)
    (D)

    The Second World Food Survey represents a more detailed and statistic-
    ally more refined analysis than the first. (See Title 89).

91. *Activities of FAO Under the Expanded Technical Assistance Pro-
    gram.* Rome 1952. 76 pp., $1.00 (D)

    Part one considers a number of selected individual projects in detail, dis-
    cusses the Food and Agriculture Organization program of various countries.

    Part two summarizes the regional projects undertaken in 1952. The
    report is illustrated, and contains statistical data.

92. *Monthly Bulletin of Agricultural Economics and Statistics.* Volume
    I, No. 1. May 1952, Rome. Annual subscription $5.00, single copy
    $0.50. (A-a) (D)

    An enlarged form of the *Monthly Bulletin of Food and Agricultural
    Statistics,* which was discontinued in April 1952. Each issue contains at

least one and sometimes several articles of concern to some phase of agricultural science, either statistical or technological. Commodity notes on various grains, meats, fats, oils, tea, tobacco, etc., follow. These notes are largely market analysis. The major part of each bulletin is devoted to statistical tables which are continuous. Data on consumption and production of various commodities, various geographical areas are given. The geographical breakdown is by political units, i.e., countries, or municipalities. The prices of selected commodities are given and census results are also included in the reports. There is no analysis of the statistical data except what is contained in the market-commodity analysis at the beginning of each *Monthly Bulletin*.

93. *Yearbook of Food and Agricultural Statistics.* Rome. First issued in 1948 for 1947. $3.50 per volume. (A-a) (A-c)

Part I — *Production.*
Part II — *Trade.*

This two part volume Yearbook continues the statistical services begun by the International Institute of Agriculture which was absorbed by the Food and Agriculture Organization in 1946. Part I — *Production*, contains statistical data on crops, livestock, employment and population. Part II — *Trade*, presents statistical information including prices of the major internationally traded agricultural products of the world.

94. *Yearbook of Forest Products Statistics.* Rome $2.50. (A-a) (A-c)

An annual statistical report beginning in 1947. Production, consumption, imports, exports, by countries of origin and countries of destination for lumber in its various phases. The report and analysis are largely in terms of quantity.

95. *Yearbook of Fisheries Statistics.* Rome. Pages vary. $3.50. (A-a) (A-c)

First issued for 1947, the second 1948-49, the third 1950-51. Covers production, consumption, foreign trade in terms of the country of origin and the country of destination. The data deal with commercial fish products. Price data are given when available. Statistical coverage begins with 1938.

96. *World Outlook and State of Food and Agriculture* (An annual first published in 1948 as *"The State of Food and Agriculture"*) Washington. Pages and prices vary. (A-a) (A-b) (D)

Presents the food and agriculture expectation of the following two year period for the world as a whole, for broad regions and for selected countries. The report also analyzes selected and individual commodities of farm, forest and sea. Developments in demand, production, marketing, consumption, and prices of agricultural products and farm incomes are also discussed. The major part of the report is analytical. There is a statistical appendix.

97. *Commodity-Policy Studies.* Rome. Pages vary. $0.50. (A-c)

These are occasional analytical studies of national and international policies for agricultural products.

98. *Commodity Reports.* Rome. Pages vary. $0.25.

These are occasional brief appraisals of the current situation in internationally traded commodities.

99. *FAO Commodity Series Bulletin.* Rome. Pages vary. $0.50. (A-a) (D)

Statistics and analysis of production, consumption, imports, exports, prices by country of origin and country of destination for various commodities as tobacco, citrus, dried fruits, grain, etc. The orientation is toward commodities rather than underdeveloped areas. The geographical breakdown gives some insight into the situation in underdeveloped areas of the commodity in question. This is an occasional series and does not have regular date of issue. To date about twenty-five Bulletins have been published.

100. *The State of Food and Agriculture.* An annual—Rome. Pages and prices vary. (A-a) (A-b (D) (See Title 96).

This annual economic survey, dating from 1951, deals with the state of food and agriculture in the world. It is made in collaboration with the member governments of the Food and Agriculture Organization and records the progress towards the chief goal of the organization to improve the nutrition, clothing, and shelter of the world. It includes surveys and outlook for all principal agricultural commodities, as well as the products of forestry and fisheries and covers the word situation, region by region.

FOOD AND AGRICULTURE ORGANIZATION—*Technical Studies*

101. *The Consolidation of Fragmented Agricultural Holdings.* Washington, 1950. 99 pp., $1.00 (A-b)

Part one describes the causes, effects and techniques for preventing fragmentation. Consolidation methods and financial considerations are described. Part two describes consolidation of agricultural holdings in Denmark, France and Switzerland. Useful as a guide to fragmentation problems in underdeveloped areas.

102. *Progress and Economic Problems of Farm Mechanization.* Washington, 1950. 88 pp., $1.00 (A-a) (A-b)

Report on production, use, trade and economic aspects of farm mechanization. Data are drawn from Europe, America, Africa and the Near and Far East.

103. *Some Aspects of Surface Water Development in Arid Regions.* Rome, 1952. 45 pp., $0.50 (A-b)

Describes some successful schemes for development of surface water in arid regions, the utilization of natural flow, storage, etc., illustrated.

104. *Land Classifications for Agricultural Development.* Rome, 1952.
38 pp., $0.50 (A-b) (D)
   A handbook for classifying land in accordance with various characteristics. Useful for taxonomic analysis.

105. *Cadastral Surveys and Records of Rights in Land.* Rome, 1953. 67
pp., $0.50. (A-b) (D)
   A report on the value and use of cadastral maps for record keeping and other more general economic uses.

106. *FAO Forestry and Forest Products Studies:*
   No. 2 — *Forest Policy, Law and Administration.* Washington — Rome, 1950, 211 pp., $2.00 (A-b) (C-3) .
   No. 3 — *Tropical Woods and Agricultural Residues as Sources of Pulp.* Rome, 1951, 190 pp., $2.00 (A-a)
   No. 4 — *Grazing and Forest Economy.* Rome, 1953, 161 pp., $2.00 (A-a) (D)
   No. 5 — *Elements of Forest Fire Control.* Rome, 1953, 110 pp., $1.00 (A-b)
   No. 6 — *Raw Materials for More Paper.* Rome, 1953, 122 pp., $2.00 (A-a) (A-b) .

107. *Fisheries Studies:*
   No. 1 — *Salted Cod and Related Species.* Washington, 1949, 196 pp., $2.00 (A-a) (A-b)
   No. 2 — *Commodity Standards for Fisheries Products.* Rome, 1953, 157 pp., $2.00 (A-b) (D)
   No. 3 — *Fisheries Bulletin.* Rome. Annual subscription $1.50, single copy $0.30. (A-a)
   Presents analyses of recent fisheries developments, economic notes, statistical tables on landings and production of certain fish and fishery commodities.

108. *FAO Development Papers*
   No. 3 — *Essential Steps in National Agricultural Development.* Washington, 1950, 16 pp., $0.25 (A-b)
   No. 5 — *Essential Considerations in the Mechanization of Farming.* Washington, 1950, 16 pp., $0.25 (A-b)
   No. 6 — *Improving Livestock Under Tropical and Sub-Tropical Conditions.* Washington, 1950, 40 pp., $0.50. (A-b)
   No. 9 — *Land Settlements for Agriculture.* Rome, 1951, 40 pp., $0.50 (A-b)
   No. 10 — *Equipment for Cleaning and Grading Seeds.* Rome, 1951, 20 pp., $0.25 (A-b)
   No. 11 — *Report of the First Meeting of the International Rice Commission's Working Party on Fertilizers.* Rome, 1951, 24 pp., $0.25 (A-b)

No. 12 — *Equipment for the Processing of Tea.* Rome, 1951, 12 pp., $0.25 (A-b)

No. 13 — *Equipment for the Tanning of Skins and Hides.* Rome, 1951, 18 pp., $0.25 (A-b)

No. 14 — *Report of the Second Meeting of the International Rice Commission's Working Party on Rice Breeding.* Rome, 1951, 82 pp., $0.50 (A-b)

No. 16 — *Agricultural Credit for Small Farmers.* Rome, 1952, 30 pp., $0.25 (A-b)

No. 17 — *Land Utilization in Tropical Areas.* Rome, 1952., 10 pp., $0.25 (A-b)

No. 18 — *Land Classification for Agriculture Development.* Rome, 1952, 38 pp., $0.50 (A-b)

No. 20 — *Farm Management Investigations for Agricultural Improvements.* Rome, 1952, 36 pp., $0.50 (A-b)

No. 21 — *Some Aspects of Surface Water Development in Arid Regions.* Rome, 1952, 45 pp., $0.50 (A-b)

No. 23 — *Digest of Plant Quarantine Regulations.* Rome, 1952, 164 pp., $2.00 (A-b)

No. 25 — *Equipment for the Ginning of Cotton.* Rome, 1953, 48 pp., $0.50 (A-b)

No. 26 — *Equipment for the Processing of Long Vegetable Fibers.* Rome, 1953, 57 pp., $0.50 (A-b)

No. 27 — *Equipment for the Processing of Rice.* Rome, 1953, 55 pp., $0.50 (A-b)

No. 28 — *Cereal Breeding Procedures.* Rome, 1952, 122 pp., $1.25 (A-b)

No. 30 — *Report of the Third Meeting of the International Rice Commission's Working Party on Rice Breeding.* Rome, 1953, 48 pp., $0.50 (A-b)

No. 31 — *Results of Co-operative Hybrid Maize Tests in European and Mediterranean Countries.* Washington, 1950, 43 pp., $0.50 (A-b)

No. 33 — *Report of the Second Inter-American Meeting on Livestock Production.* Rome, 1953, 183 pp., $1.50 (A-b)

109. *FAO Agricultural Studies*

No. 1 — *Breeding Livestock Adapted to Unfavorable Environments.* Washington, 1948, 176 pp., and bibliography, $1.50 (A-b)

No. 4 — *Soil Conservation — An International Study.* Washington, 1948, 189 pp., $2.00 (A-b)

No. 9 — *Efficient Use of Fertilizers.* Washington, 1952, 182 pp., $2.00 (A-b)

No. 11 — *Consolidation of Fragmented Agricultural Holdings.* Washington, 1950, 69 pp., maps, table, $1.00 (A-b)

No. 16 — *Improving the World's Grasslands.* Rome, 1951, 147 pp., $2.00 (A-b)

No. 17 — *Communal Land Tenure.* Rome, 1953, 57 pp., $0.50 (A-b)

No. 18 — *Cadastral Surveys and Records of Rights in Land.* Rome, 1953, 64 pp., $0.50 (A-b)

No. 19 — *Zebu Cattle of India and Pakistan*. Washington, 1946, 250 pp., $2.50 (A-b)

No. 20 — *Soil Surveys for Land Development*. Rome, 1953, 100 pp., $1.00 (A-b)

No. 21 — *Legumes in Agriculture*. Rome, 1953, 367 pp., $3.00. Bibliography and appendices. (A-b)

110. *FAO Nutritional Studies*

No. 1 — *Rice and Rice Diets*. Washington, 1948, 72 pp., $0.75 (A-b)

No. 2 — *Synthetic Fats*. Washington, 1949, 14 pp., $0.25 (A-b)

No. 3 — *Food Composition Tables for International Use*. Washington, 1949, 56 pp., $0.75 (A-b)

No. 4 — *Dietary Surveys: Their Technique and Interpretations*. Washington, 1949, 108 pp., $1.00 (A-b)

No. 5 — *Calory Requirements*. Washington, 1950, 65 pp., $0.75 (A-b)

No. 6 — *Teaching Better Nutrition*. Washington, 1950, 148 pp., $1.50 (A-b)

No. 7 — *Nutrition Work in Greece*. Rome, 1951, 67 pp., $0.50 (A-b)

No. 9 — *Maize and Maize Diets*. Rome, 1953, 94 pp., $1.00 (A-b)

111. *Unasylva*—pages vary. Rome. $2.50 per year, $0.65 per issue. (A-a)

Quarterly review of forestry and forest products. Contains articles, conference reports, commodity reports, and reviews of technical literature. Subscribers receive *Forestry and Forest Products* — a bibliography.

112. *World Fisheries Abstracts*. Rome. Annual subscription $4.00; single copy $0.75. (A-b)

A bimonthly review of technical literature of fisheries and related industries. Covers the field of fisheries technology, processing methods, boat design, fishing methods, chemical examination of fisheries products, etc.

Food and Agricultural Organization—*Regional Studies*

113. *Prospects for Agricultural Development in Latin America*. Food and Agriculture Organization. Rome (Undated), 146 pp., $1.00. (A-b)

A discussion of developments in food and agriculture in Latin America. Production, consumption and trade are analyzed. It covers farm mechanization, fisheries and forestry development as well. The study is conducted on a country by country and commodity by commodity basis. Tables and charts are included.

114. *Report of the FAO Mission for Greece*. Washington, 1947. 188 pp., $1.50. (A-a) (A-b)

Basic orientation is to expose the agricultural and fisheries resources, and to make recommendations for increased production.

The study also deals with problems of general economic development including considerations of education, health, civil service, and taxation. Illustrated.

115. *Report of the Mission for Siam.* Washington, 1948. 125 pp., $1.50
   (A-a) (A-b)

   An illustrated report discussing agricultural production, irrigation, forestry, insect control and recommendations for improvements. A bibliography is included.

116. *Report of the FAO Mission to Nicaragua.* Washington and Rome,
   1950. 200 pp., $2.00. (A-a) (A-b) (D)

   Covers agricultural resources and development, including forestry crop
   and grassland production. Recommendations for reform and improvement
   are made. The report is illustrated and there is appended a bibliography
   and statistical information regarding climate, and rainfall by provinces.

117. *Report of the Meeting on Fertilizer Production, Distribution and
   Utilization in Latin America.* 1951. 52 pp., $0.50. (A-b) (D)

   Deals with the technique and economics of fertilizer use, production, and
   distribution in Latin American Countries. The unit of investigation is the
   nation.

118. *Agriculture in Asia and the Far East, Development and Outlook.*
   Food and Agriculture Organization. Rome, 1953. 163 pp., $1.00.
   (A-b) (D)

   Part I consists of the Report of the Food and Agriculture Organization
   Regional Meeting on Food and Agricultural Programs and Outlook in
   Asia and the Far East. It discusses the current status of agriculture, fisheries, forestry, etc. Economic and financial measures to encourage development, and government services to agriculture are analyzed.

   Part II discusses the development of land and water resources, and programs for crop and livestock improvement problems and programs for
   fisheries and forests. It is conducted on a country by country basis, and
   includes statistical tables.

119. *Agriculture in the Near East, Development and Outlook.* Rome,
   1953. 78 pp., $1.00. (A-a) (D)

   Reviews the work of the Second (Near East) Regional Meeting of the
   Food and Agriculture Organization held in Cairo 1-9 September, 1953.
   It analyzes the development of agriculture from 1951, including development programs, food consumption, technical aspects of farming, price
   policies and social welfare. A list of delegates to the meeting is included.

INTERNATIONAL BANK FOR RECONSTRUCTION AND DEVELOPMENT

120. *The Basis of a Development Program for Colombia.* International
   Bank for Reconstruction and Development, Washington, D.C.,
   1950. 642 pp., $5.00. (A-a) (A-b) (C)

   Divided into two parts; part one entitled "The Problem," analyzes the
   economic resources, and the fiscal, financial, educational, health and organizational aspects of the economy and government. Part two entitled.

The Program recommends projects and details of procedure for the economic and social development of the country. The final chapter entitled "The Overall Program and Its Implementation" summarizes the program and its course.

121. *The Economic Development of Guatemala*. Johns Hopkins Press, Baltimore, 1951. 305 pp., $5.00. (A-a) (A-b) (D)

Examines and appraises the economic resources and financial resources of Guatemala. An investment program is recommended and capital accumulation is specifically discussed.

122. *The Economy of Turkey—An Analysis and Recommendations for a Development Program*. International Bank for Reconstruction and Development, Washington, 1951. 276 pp., $5.00 (A-a) (C)

Deals with the economic administration of Turkey as well as the major economic problems confronting that economy. The resources and potential of agriculture, industry, transportation, mining, and such non-economic matters as education, public health, public administration, financial organization are examined.

It also contains a set of recommendations designed to expedite the economic development of the Turkish economy.

A summary of the report of the mission was published as the *Economy of Turkey—an Analysis and Recommendations for a Development Program, Summary of the Report of a Mission*, International Bank for Reconstruction and Development, Washington, D. C., 87 pp.

123. *Report on Cuba. Economic and Technical Mission to Cuba*. International Bank for Reconstruction and Development. Washington, 1951. 1052 pp., $7.50. (A-a) (A-b) (D)

A detailed analysis of the economy of Cuba with suggested policies for the more important economic problems.

It includes agriculture and animal husbandry, mining, industry, power and other public services, transportation, internal commerce, availability and utilization of labor, local capital resources and the mechanisms for channeling them into productive investment, foreign trade and exchange, monetary policies and other economic and financial policies effecting development. It is analytical rather than statistical, although statistics are provided to support the analysis.

124. *The Agricultural Development of Uruguay*. International Bank for Reconstruction and Development and Food and Agriculture Organization. Washington, 1951. 231 pp., Mimeographed. No price. (A-a) (A-b) (D)

Prepared by a joint commission sent to Uruguay by the IBRD and the FAO of the United Nations. It is a technical report dealing with ways and means to better land use in Uruguay with special reference to pastoral activities. Technical recommendations are given not only in the field of land use, but also on such economic problems as marketing, prices, capital requirements, etc.

125. *The Economic Development of Iraq.* Johns Hopkins Press, Baltimore, 1952, 463 pp., $5.00. (A-a) (A-b) (D)

    The first part contains the major findings and recommendations of the International Bank Mission to Iraq. The analysis of the resources of the country are discussed generally. The second part consists of a series of monographic studies dealing with particular problems e.g. flood control, drainage, agriculture, animal husbandry, education, community planning.

126. *Surinam, Recommendations for a Ten Year Development Program.* Johns Hopkins Press, Baltimore, 1952. 271 pp., $5.00. (A-a) (A-b) (D)

    Analyzes the basic features and history of the Surinam economy and then develops a program of development in the light of the resources of the economy. It is detailed and the recommendations are quite specific. It deals primarily with economics, trade and production.

127. *The Agricultural Economy of Chile.* International Bank for Reconstruction and Development and Food and Agriculture Organization. Washington, 1952. Mimeographed. 353 pp., No price. (A-a) (A-b) (D)

    Prepared by a joint International Bank for Reconstruction and Development and Food and Agricultural Organization Mission; primarily examines the Chilean agricultural economy. Recommendations are made for agricultural developments. The analysis and recommendations are administrative as well as economic, financial and technical. Relations of the agricultural and non-agricultural aspects of the economy are considered.

128. *The Economic Development of Jamaica.* Johns Hopkins Press, Baltimore, 1952. 288 pp., $5.00. (A-a) (A-b) (C) (D)

    Deals with the resources and development potential of Jamaica. The first part of the report analyzes the agricultural and manufacturing potential of the economy and examines the problems of financing such development. The second part presents statistics of production, and analyzes the credit, land and industrial relations institutions of the Island. Governmental and public institutions bearing on the economic development are also analyzed.

129. *The Economic Development of Ceylon.* Johns Hopkins Press. Baltimore, 1953. 829 pp., $7.50. (A-a) (A-b) (B-1) (C) (D)

    A report on economic development and potential of Ceylon prepared by the staff of the International Bank. The economic resources including the human resources are analyzed and the productive activity potential of the economy is examined in detail. Sections on public health, technology, education, fiscal policy, etc., are included. Detailed recommendations are made.

130. *The Economic Development of Mexico. Combined Mexican Working Party.* Johns Hopkins Press, Baltimore, 1953. 392 pp., $10.00. (A-a) (A-b) (D)

This very complete statistical and analytical report on Mexico includes discussion of the national income for 1940-1950, the economics of agriculture, livestock, forestry, fisheries, mining, petroleum, electric power industry, transportation and communication, education, public health and welfare, public finance, balance of payments, and outlines the prospects and potential of the Mexican economy. It is done in great detail with abundance of statistics, most of which are time series.

131. *The Economic Development of Nicaragua.* Johns Hopkins Press, Baltimore, 1953. 424 pp., $5.00. (A-a) (A-b) (C)
The orientation is mainly toward the development of the Nicaraguan economy. The developmental potential of the various sectors of the economy is discussed, as are the problems and policies of development.
Details of mining, roads, ports, postal, telegraph, telephone service, agriculture and government fiscal policies are discussed. Recommendations of specific sorts are made.

BOOKS AND PERIODICALS

1. ABRAMOWITZ, Moses. *The Economics of Growth*, "A Survey of Contemporary Economics," Vol. II, Haley ed., Illinois 1952. (A-b) (A-c) (D)
Summarizes the scope of recent literature dealing with economic growth. Stresses the role of entrepreneurship, and discusses capital formation as a cause of growth in relation to the following variables: the influence of savings; the productivity of capital; the role of finance; and the outlook for investment opportunities in already developed economies.

2. ADLER, J. H. "Fiscal and Monetary Implementation of Development Programs," *American Economic Review, Papers and Proceedings,* May 1952. (A) (b)
Stresses the importance of creating external economies and social overhead capital, and the implications of this need for the size of the investment required in the early stages of development. Discusses specific fiscal and monetary policy designed to achieve determined investment goals.

3. ADLER, J. H. *The Underdeveloped Areas: Their Industrialization,* Yale Institute of International Studies, New Haven, 1949. (A) (c)
Appraises the present state of industrialization and the presumably narrow role of private enterprise in the initial process.

4. ADY, P. H. "Britain and Overseas Development" in *The British Economy* 1945-50. The Clarendon Press—Oxford, Page 550 ff.
A factual account of British foreign, especially Empire, trade of the recent past. The nature, regulation, restrictions, and volume of the trade are analyzed.

5. ALLEN, G. C. *A Short Economic History of Modern Japan*, London, 1946. (B) (C)
Concentrates on the emergence of modern industrial society in Japan since 1868. Discusses the characteristics of Tokugawa Japan and the factors which contributed to the subsequent course of Japanese growth.

6. AUBREY, H. G. "Deliberate Industrialization," *Social Research*, June 1949. (A) (b)
Stresses the role of government in economic development with particular reference to industrialization in Mexico. Notes the necessity for external economies requiring government assistance, and points out that such assistance was common to all the countries of Western Europe, to the United States and, in extreme degree, to Japan.

7. AUBREY, H. G. *Industrial Enterprise in Underdeveloped Countries*, Universities-National Bureau Committee for Economic Research (unpublished paper), November, 1953. (A) (b)
A discussion of entrepreneurship in underdeveloped areas, with particular emphasis on the role of uncertainty and the lack of precedent in deterring emergence of entrepreneurship and acceleration of capital formation.

8. AUBREY, H. G. "Small Industry in Economic Development," *Social Research*, September, 1951. (A) (b)
An analysis of the economic and social case for small industries. Noting the typical scarcity of capital in underdeveloped economies, emphasizes that small local industries may increase capital supply which would not be available for large-scale investment. Also stresses the capital-saving characteristics of small industries in terms of a typically low capital-output ratio, and the avoidance of capital-intensive overhead costs usually associated with centralized, urbanized industries.

9. BALGOOYEN, H. W. "Experience of United States Private Business in Latin America," *American Economic Review, Papers and Proceedings*, May, 1951. (A) (c)
Discusses briefly the history of American private investment in Latin America, and the changed attitudes that have marked this history.

10. BAUGH, W. H. "Capital Formation and Entrepreneurship in the South," *Southern Economic Journal*, October, 1949. (B)
Discusses the slow rate of capital formation and growth in the South and attempts to account for this anomaly in terms of a comparison of economic, cultural and social factors.

11. BLOCK, E. "United States Foreign Investment and the Dollar Shortage," *Review of Economics and Statistics*, May, 1953. (A) (c)
Points out that typically American foreign investment attention is attracted to dollar export industries which, generally, are not the industries lacking capital resources.

12. BOHR, K. A. "Investment Criteria for Manufacturing Industries in Underdeveloped Countries," *Review of Economics and Statistics,* May, 1954 (A) (b)

Starts from the premise that scarcity of capital, shortage of skilled labor, scattered location and small size of market are four major limiting factors on investment in manufacturing industries in underdeveloped countries. Proceeds to devise methods for measuring various industries in terms of these criteria as a guide to investment decision-making.

13. BOULDING, K. E. "Religious Foundations of Economic Progress," *Harvard Business Review,* May, 1952. (B)

Emphasizes the role of cultural institutions and processes in either perpetuating poverty or in stimulating change, especially by the incentives afforded indigenous entrepreneurship.

14. BRITNELL, G. E. "Factors in the Economic Development of Guatemala," *American Economic Review, Papers and Proceedings,* May, 1953. (A) (b)

Discusses obstacles to capital formation and investment with emphasis on political instability, bias toward labor in disputes with management, alternative investment opportunities from speculation, mortgages and trade.

15. BROZEN, Y. "Determinants of the Direction of Technological Changes, *American Economic Review, Papers and Proceedings,* May, 1953. (A) (b)

Sets forth the idea that technological change is an endogenous variable, and that the types of technological change developed by a given society are influenced in part by the character, availability and relative price of its resources, and the relative growth rates of different industries.

16. BROZEN, Y. "Determinants of Entrepreneurial Ability," *Social Research,* Autumn 1954. (A) (B) (b)

Attributes to the entrepreneur the function of applying new technology to available resources and thereby assuring maximum productivity of new capital formation. Deals with the following factors affecting the quality and quantity of creative entrepreneurship: the prevailing religious ethic; the existence of extremes of social rigidity; recruiting and training practices; the stream of "new men" coming into the entrepreneurial sphere; society's rewards to entrepreneurs; ready access of entrepreneurs to capital.

17. BROZEN, Y. "Invention, Innovation and Imitation," *American Economic Review, Papers and Proceedings,* May, 1951. (A) (b)

In discussing the role of technological change in economic development, it is shown that given inventions may be economic for some resource situations but not for others. Suggests that the proper direction of research in underdeveloped areas may be in terms of "raising technological possibilities for the area" rather than the importation of technological know-how developed abroad.

18. BUCHANAN, D. H. "Japan Versus Asia," *American Economic Review, Papers and Proceedings,* May, 1951. (B)
    Discusses the causes of economic growth in Japan in contrast to the trend of development in other Asian countries.

19. BUCHANAN, D. H. *The Development of Capitalistic Enterprise in India,* Cambridge, 1934. (A) (B) (b)
    A thorough but dated account of the growth of commercial and industrial activities in India; includes discussion of social and cultural values, the record of growth in specific industries, and especially the role of business leadership and of the managing agent system.

20. CHANG, Pei-kang. *Agriculture and Industrialization,* Cambridge, 1949. (A) (b)
    The impact of industrialization on agriculture. The analysis is divided into four sections covering the relationship between industrialization and agricultural reform, the problem of balance between these two sectors in an expanding economy, the relationship between older industrialized and newer industrializing economies, and the problems of industrialization confronting Japan.

21. CHENERY, H. H., and CLARK, P. G. *Structure and Growth of the Italian Economy,* Mutual Security Agency, Rome, 1953. (A) (a) (b)
    An input-output study of Italy. It provides both basic data on Italian economic interrelationships, and a methodological guide for the analysis of income generation and flow.

22. CHIANG, Hsieh. "Underdevelopment in Asia: Its Relation to Investment Policy," *International Labour Review,* July, 1952. (A) (b)
    Discusses some of the broader social aspects of capital formation in Asia, in relation to the investment programs being followed. Emphasizes the need for small-scale rural industries and for applying innovations which will make possible new methods of production, differing both from large-scale and cottage industries.

23. CLARK, Colin. "World Resources and World Population," *Economia Internazionale,* Vol. IV, Genoa, 1951. (A) (a) (b)
    Argues that food shortages are generally due, in a global sense, to labor shortages in agriculture. Food is not a limiting factor in world development. Population will increase slightly in the future but food prices will also increase relative to other prices, stimulating production areas.

24. CLARK, Colin. "Population Growth and Living Standards," *International Labor Review,* Vol. LXVII No. 2, Geneva, August, 1953. (A) (a) (b)
    A long run analysis of potential food supplies and population. The analysis suggests the economic conditions which are required if the world is to provide a rising standard of living for the underdeveloped sectors of the world economy.

25. CLARK, J. M. "Common and Disparate Elements in National Growth and Decline," *Problems in the Study of Economic Growth,* Universities—National Bureau Committee for Economic Research, July, 1949 (D).
Defines the concept of growth as distinguished from qualitative progress and formulates tentative hypotheses to serve as a guide for future research.

26. CLARK, S. D. "Religion and Economic Backward Areas," *American Economic Review, Papers and Proceedings,* May, 1952 (B)
Concentrates on the relationship between the rise of Protestantism and industrialization, with heavy reliance on Weber and Tawney.

27. COHEN, J. B. "Private Point Four in Japan," *Fortune,* April, 1953. (A) (c)
Discusses the methods used by Japan since 1950 to attract private foreign investment.

28. CUMPER, G. E. "Labor Productivity and Capital-Labor Ratio in Jamaican manufacturing industries: Their relation to the Problem of Selective Industrialization," *Social and Economic Studies,* February, 1953. (A) (a) (B) (b)
Using 1946 statistics, differences among industries are analyzed in terms of such factors as average annual wage, average net production per worker, value of fixed capital per worker. Conclusions are advanced concerning types of industries considered most advantageous in capital-poor, labor-rich countries.

29. DAVIS, K. "Population and Change in Backward Areas," *Columbia Journal of International Affairs,* Spring, 1950. (A) (a)
The demographic problems of underdeveloped areas are discussed in relation to statistics of population density, income, literacy and urbanization. Doubts are expressed that migration, population control or rapid industrialization, or all three together can contribute to a smooth transition to economic betterment.

30. DIAMOND, W. "The Industrial Development Bank of Turkey," *The Middle East Journal,* July, 1950. (A) (c)
A description of the formation of the Industrial Development Bank and an outline of its function, sources of funds and their significance.

31. DORE, R. P. "Japanese Rural Fertility: Some Social and Economic Factors," *Population Studies,* July, 1953. (A) (a)
Long and short-range trends in factors affecting rural fertility are discussed, including changes in attitudes of rural inhabitants toward birth control.

32. ELLSWORTH, P. T. "Factors in the Economic Development of Ceylon," *American Economic Review, Papers and Proceedings,* May, 1953. (B)
Cultural and social obstacles to industrial growth are discussed with particular emphasis on the problem of population growth.

33. FABRICANT, S. "Some Factors Affecting the Prospects of Foreign Investment," *The Analysts Journal,* November, 1952. (A) (c)
Discusses the effect on short and long range prospects for United States investment abroad, including such factors as the defaults of the 1920's; the speed and pattern of development desired by the underdeveloped countries, etc.

34. FINE, S. M. *Japan's Post-War Industrial Recovery,* Foreign Affairs Association of Japan, 1953. (A) (b)
Analyzes the recovery of Japan's industry, especially in respect to the policy of SCAP and the Japanese Government.

35. FRANKEL, S. H. *Capital Investment in Africa,* Oxford, 1938. (A) (c)
A historical analysis of the role and character of capital investment in Africa through the early 1930's, with a statistical presentation of the amounts, kinds and returns on investment in different countries in the continent.

36. GERSCHENKRON, A. "Social Attitudes, Entrepreneurship and Economic Development," *Explorations in Entrepreneurial History,* Cambridge, 1953. (A) (B) (b)
A brief review of theories concerning the effect of the prevailing climate of opinion upon the quality and quantity of entrepreneurship. Based on recent French and German experiences, it is tentatively suggested that social attitudes hostile to the entrepreneur do not significantly affect the process of growth if they are not crystallized in adverse government action.

37. Government of India. *Report of the Rural Banking Inquiry Committee,* New Delhi, 1950. (A) (c)
Explores the possibility of increasing rural banking facilities in India for the purpose of mobilizing rural savings. Also examines changes in rural income since 1930.

38. Government of Pakistan. *The Public Investment Inquiry Report,* Karachi, 1951. (A) (c) (A)
Examines the principal obstacles to increased foreign investment in terms of heavy incidence of taxation, conflict between commerce and industry, the unfamiliarity with joint stock corporate organizations, inadequate banking facilities, etc.

39. HAAVELMO, T. *A Study in the Theory of Economic Evolution,* Amsterdam, 1954. (A)

A theoretical approach to explaining the widely variant historical growth rates. Stresses the cumulative impact of small differences in initial conditions and of random "shocks."

40. HOSELITZ, B. F. *Entrepreneurship and Capital Formation in France and Britain since 1700.* Universities—National Bureau for Economic Research. (unpublished paper). November, 1953. (A) (b)
A comparative study of French and British economic development, dealing with institutions affecting capital formation and use, forms of entrepreneurship and sources and magnitude of capital formation.

41. HOSELITZ, B. F. "Entrepreneurship and Economic Growth," *American Journal of Economics and Sociology,* October, 1952. (A) (b)
An analysis of personality factors affecting economic activities in general and capital formation in particular, and the relation of personality factors to social structure.

42. HOSELITZ, B. F. "Non-Economic Barriers to Economic Development," *Economic Development and Cultural Change,* March, 1952. (B)
Discusses such non-economic barriers to capital formation as lack of social mobility, adverse value systems, monopoly of social prestige by one group, etc.

43. HUGGINS, H. D. "Employment, Economic Development and Incentive Financing in Jamaica," *Social and Economic Studies,* February, 1953. (A) (c)
Methods of stimulating capital formation and industrialization are discussed in terms of promotional activities, methods of incentive financing and the mobilization of "centers of funds and entrepreneurship", etc.

44. HUNTER, J. M. "Long-term Foreign Investment and Underdeveloped Countries," *Journal of Political Economy,* February, 1953. (A) (c)
The characteristics of direct investment and the attitude of underdeveloped countries towards such investment are analyzed.

45. JOHNSON, V. W. and METCALF, J. E. "Land Redistribution and Industrial Development," *Land Economics,* May, 1953. (A) (c)
Presents a plan for combining land redistribution with transfers of wealth from land to industrial capital.

46. KAHN, A. E. "Investment Criteria in Development Programs," *Quarterly Journal of Economics,* February, 1951. (A) (b) (A) (c)
Discusses three criteria related to the selection of investment projects: the capital intensity criterion; the export-increasing or import-reducing nature of the product; and the direct versus indirect foreign exchange requirements of new investments.

47. KERWIN, R. W. "Private Enterprise in Turkish Industrial Development," *Middle East Journal,* Winter, 1951. (A) (b) (c) (B)
The adverse effects of "étatisme" on private industrial development, are noted, as well as the following factors: scarcity of capital for private investment, high rates of interest, high rate of return on commercial enterprises which discourages industrial investment, tendency of industry to engage in speculation and build high inventories.

48. KERWIN, R. W. "The Turkish Roads Program," *The Middle East Journal,* April, 1950. (B)
A particular investment project considered in terms of the various cultural obstacles encountered and the solutions developed for dealing with them.

49. KINDELBERGER, C. P. "Review of the I.B.R.D. Monographs on Turkey, Guatemala and Cuba," *Review of Economics and Statistics,* November, 1952. (A)
Describes the I.B.R.D. reports as being "essays in comparative statics." Kindelberger claims that the reports attempt to solve the problem of what should be done in the country as a whole, rather than focusing on the highest priorities and smallest number of projects which would form the basis of a self-sustaining economy. In his view, the key factors in the process of development are: the market and money economy, capital formation, and the process of innovation.

50. KURESHI, A. T. *Islam and the Theory of Interest,* Lahore, 1946. (B)
Examines Islamic objections to the charging and receipt of interest in the light of interest theory.

51. KUZNETS, S. S. "Suggestion for an Inquiry into the Economic Growth of Nations," *Problems in the Study of Economic Growth,* Universities—National Bureau Committee on Economic Research, July, 1949. (D)
Explains need for limiting scope of research to particular countries, covering a specified time period and dealing with "historico-statistical comparisons."

52. LACKDAWALA, D. T. *International Aspects of India in Economic Development,* Oxford, 1951. (A) (b) (c)
Problems of foreign capital investment in India are analyzed, and the view expressed that foreign direct capital investment should be welcomed, but efforts should be taken to ensure that such capital is channelled into socially advantageous uses and that no transfer problems arise.

53. League of Nations, *Statistics relating to Capital Formation* (Studies and reports on statistical methods) Geneva, 1938. (A) (a)
Briefly describes the process of capital formation and stresses the difficulties of measuring such concepts as savings and investment, as contrasted with quantities of physical capital.

54. MOORE, W. E. "Primitives and Peasants in Industry," *Social Research*, March, 1948. (A) (a)
Political, economic, psychological and social pressures and incentives affecting labor mobility in underdeveloped areas are analyzed.

55. MOORE, W. E. *Utilization of Human Resources through Industrialization*, Milbank Memorial Fund, 1950. (A) (a) (B)
Discusses industrialization in general with particular reference to labor mobility. Doubts that wage differentials or other "incentives" are likely to be sufficiently strong to promote labor mobility in underdeveloped countries. Suggests that various "pressures" in addition to incentives are needed to promote labor mobility. Land shortage and displacement of handicraft by cheap manufactures are examples of such pressures. These hypotheses are related to field work in Mexico.

56. MOSK, S. A. "Latin America Versus the United States," *American Economic Review, Papers and Proceedings,* May, 1951. (B)
Analysis considers social structure as influencing differential economic progress.

57. MYINT, H. "Economic Backwardness," *Oxford Economic Papers,* Oxford University Press, 1951. (A) (a)
Economic and related factors as they affect capital formation and development. Prices, costs and capital returns are considered.

58. National Industrial Conference Board—*Capital Formation and Its Elements,* New York, 1939. (A)
Contains eight articles on capital formation which analyze various aspects of the subject, including the effect of tax policy on capital formation, the growth of large corporations and its effects on capital formation, etc. All of the articles view the problem of capital formation from the standpoint of modern industrialized economies in a depression situation.

59. National Industrial Conference Board, *Obstacles to Direct Foreign Investment,* April, 1951. (A) (c)
Uses a questionnaire approach to identify empirically the obstacles which American investors believe deter them from foreign investment. Major obstacles cited by the respondents include export or import quotas: limitations on private remittances: control of capital movements, etc.

60. NURKSE, R. *Problems of Capital Formation in Underdeveloped Countries,* Oxford, 1953. (A) (a) (b)
A comprehensive theoretical discussion of problems of capital formation. Nurkse emphasizes the influence of the "demonstration effect" and of underemployment in reducing the supply of savings; and stresses the role of limited market size and the technological discontinuities of new investments as limitations on the demand for capital. Consideration is given to the relation between commercial policy and capital formation, and the role of social overhead.

61. PAN, Yu-Pu. *International Capital Movements and Capital Forma-tion*, Urbana, Ill., 1948, pamphlet. (A) (c)
Analyzes the economic impact of international capital movements on bor-rowing and lending countries, with particular attention to China and the United States.

62. PERLOFF, H. *Puerto Rico's Economic Future*, Chicago. 1950. (A) (c) (c)
A comprehensive review and evaluation of Puerto Rico's economic devel-opment is presented. The use of tax incentives and other fiscal devices to attract new industrial capital are considered.

63. REUBENS, E. P. "A Comment on 'Factors in Economic Develop-ment'" *American Economic Review, Papers and Proceedings*, May, 1953. (A)
An interdisciplinary approach to problems of development conceived in terms of four key variables: the economic circumstances; production func-tions; socio-economic propensities; and socio-economic structure. It is sug-gested that problems of capital formation can be satisfactorily analyzed in these terms.

64. REUBENS, E. P. *Foreign Capital in Economic Development: A Case Study of Japan*. Milbank Memorial Fund, New York, 1950. (A) (c)
Notes that only limited use was made of foreign capital in Japanese devel-opment and that generally such capital was in the form of loans to the Government rather than private investments. Japan's development is attri-buted to (a) careful and effective use of the capital that was borrowed (including emphasis on capital-light industries with short maturation period) and (b) full use of domestic capital potentialities.

65. ROSENSTEIN-RODAN, P. N. "Problems of Industrialization of Eastern and South Eastern Europe," *Economic Journal*, June-September, 1943. (A) (b)
The role of the state in industrialization in this region is noted, as is the problem of achieving complementarity of different industries and external economies by a sufficiently large-scale initial industrialization.

66. ROSTOW, W. W. *The Process of Economic Growth*, New York, 1952. (B) (D)
Presents a theoretical framework for organizing and analyzing hypotheses and data related to economic growth in terms of six propensities, repre-senting the "variables of the human response to economic development."

67. SAWYER, J. E. "Social Stucture and Economic Progress," *American Economic Review, Papers and Proceedings*, May, 1951. (B)
That economic processes should be conceived as a function of total social structure in order to answer key questions concerning economic growth is the thesis of this study.

68. SCHLESINGER, E. R. *Multiple Exchange Rates and Economic Development*, Princeton, 1952. (A) (c)
Discusses the use of multiple exchange rates to discourage non-essential imports and encourage essential ones, and in general to alter the distribution of income as between consumption and investment.

69. SCHUMPETER, E. B. (ed.) *The Industrialization of Japan and Manchukuo 1930-1940*, MacMillan, 1940. (A) (b)
G. C. Allen analyzes the organization of industries in Japan and discusses the background, development, and organizational forms characterizing four main industrial groups.

70. SCHURR, S. G. and MARSHAK, J. *Economic Aspects of Atomic Power*, Princeton, 1950. (A) (b)
A survey of the subject, containing useful data on the economic characteristics of atomic power and its possible implications for development and capital requirements in underdeveloped areas.

71. SEERS, Dudley. "The Role of National Income Estimates in the Statistical Policy of an Underdeveloped Area," *Review of Economic Studies*, Vol. XX (3) No. 53. (A) (a)
Analyzes the use of statistics in planning, and suggests that specific rather than aggregative data are more useful for an underdeveloped economy's planning.

72. SINGER, H. W. "Economic Progress in Underdeveloped Countries," *Social Research*, March, 1949. (A) (c)
Analyzes obstacles to growth arising from the terms of trade and discusses the vicious-circle characteristics of such obstacles in underdeveloped economies.

73. SPENGLER, J. J. "Sociological Value Theory, Economic Analyses and Economic Policy," *American Economic Review, Papers and Proceedings*, May, 1953. (B)
The possibility of incorporating value analysis into the context of "manipulative economics" to accelerate development is considered. The role of different value systems which hinder growth is stressed. Suggests an analysis of circumstances that have led in the past to the acceptance of favorable values in replacement of adverse values.

74. SPENGLER, J. J. "The Population Obstacle to Economic Betterment," *American Economic Review, Papers and Proceedings*, May, 1951. (A)
The role of capital formation and entrepreneurship, as factors in the industrialization necessary to reduce rates of population growth in underdeveloped countries, is the focus of this paper.

75. SPICER, E. H. (ed.) *Human Problems in Technological Change,* New York, 1952. (B)
Contains a series of case studies of attempts to bring about change in a variety of cultures with varying methods and results.

76. STALEY, E. *The Future of Underdeveloped Countries—Political Implications of Economic Development,* New York, 1954. (C)
A broad discussion of the political consequences of economic development. Of particular interest are the sections which discuss the political implications of alternative methods of increasing the supply of and the demand for capital, and the political significance of foreign investment in the underdeveloped areas.

77. SUBBA RAO, G. V. "The Impact of Industrialization on Indian Society," *Columbia Journal of International Affairs,* Spring, 1950. (B)
The history of industrialization in India and its effect on the joint family, the caste system and the village is summarized.

78. SVIMEZ (Editorial and Publishing Association) *Economic Effects of an Investment Program in Southern Italy.* Rome, 1951. (A) (c)
A detailed analysis of the effects of an investment program in Southern Italy, with particular emphasis on the balance of payments repercussions of the proposed investment program.

79. SYED, H. A. *Report on the Need and the Supply of Credit in the Rural Areas of Punjab,* Board of Economic Inquiry, Lahore, 1951. (A) (c)
A sample study of the sources and needs for credit in rural areas in the Punjab. It examines the disappearance of the Hindu money-lender with Partition, and discusses the emergence of new sources and forms of credit.

80. TAEUBER, I. B. *Population and Manpower in Japan,* Milbank Memorial Fund, New York, 1950. (A) (a)
Japan's population history is analyzed and the similarities between Japan's experiences and that of western countries during the course of their industrialization are discussed. The effect of industrialization in reducing the rate of population growth is stressed.

81. TAX, S. "Selective Cultural Change," *American Economic Review, Papers and Proceedings,* May, 1951. (B)
Argues that it is possible, though not probable, to change cultures selectively in stimulating economic growth.

82. THOMPSON, S. H. "Social Aspects of Rural Industrialization," *Milbank Memorial Fund Quarterly,* July, 1948. (B)
The need to apply new technology in rural industry, within the framework of existing attitudes and social structures, is considered.

83. THORNBURG, Max, SOULE, George, et al., *Turkey: an Economic Appraisal,* The Twentieth Century Fund, 1949. (A) (b)
An extensive study of government and private policies related to social development. Legal, tax and other obstacles to private initiative are noted and specific instances based on personal interviews are cited. Stress is placed on the need for building up a pool of skilled managers and planners rather than for money capital.

84. THORNER, D. "Great Britain and the Development of India's Railways," *Journal of Economic History,* Fall, 1951. (A) (b)
Describes the effect of British organization and management policies in limiting the impact of railway development on Indian industrialization.

85. United States Department of Commerce, *Study of Factors Limiting American Private Foreign Investment,* July, 1953. (A) (c)
A general and preliminary summary of the findings of an on-going study. The findings particularly emphasize effects of trade and exchange controls, economic nationalism, political instability, and low levels of economic development.

86. VAN SICKLE, J. V. "A Case Study in Delayed Industrialization," *American Economic Review, Papers and Proceedings,* May, 1951. (A)
Delayed industrialization of the South Eastern United States, and the measures that have been used with some success to stimulate growth, are discussed.

87. WOODS, B. J. P. "South Africa's Finance Corporation," *The Banker,* September, 1953. (A) (c)
The Corporation's activities are evaluated in terms of its declared objective, i.e. the mobilization of idle capital, the attraction of foreign capital, and the cooperation of different financial institutions within the country.

88. WOOD, R. and KEYSER, V. *United States Business Performance Abroad: Sears Roebuck de Mexico, S.A.,* National Planning Association, May, 1953. (A) (c)
First of a series of case studies of particular American business investments abroad. It emphasizes the effect of Mexico's import tax in stimulating domestic investment, and the role of Sears' management techniques in developing local sources of supply and thereby stimulating indigenous capital formation.

CURRENT RESEARCH

1. Allahabad University, Department of Economics, *Studies of Industrial Growth in India.* (A) (b)
   On-going studies by research scholars at the University on various aspects of industrial growth. Includes several studies of particular industries and some work on the impact of taxation on investment.

2. Bombay University, School of Economics and Sociology, *Research Studies on Industrial Development.* (A) (b)
   On-going studies by research scholars of particular industries with emphasis on the role of capital formation in their growth.

3. Chicago, University of, *Evaluation of Technical Assistance Programs in Latin America* (T. Schultz, Director) (D)
   A research project now under way, which will involve an evaluation of the socio-economic impact of public, private, bi-lateral and multilateral technical assistance in Mexico and other Latin American countries. Efforts will also be made to measure the effect of different kinds of technical assistance on the rate and kinds of capital formation in particular countries.

4. Chicago, University of, *Research Center in Economic Development and Cultural Change* (H. Perloff, Director) (Entire Outline)
   Presently studying a broad range of conceptual and factual problems in the field of economic development, including an inventory of economic development and political change, a comparison of Western and non-Western conceptions of economic development, and a complete analysis of problems of mobilizing human resources in underdeveloped areas in relation to new capital formation. The Center's current work will also investigate foreign influences on the development and behavior of entrepreneural elites by case studies of Indian, Turkish and Japanese experiences.

5. Cornell University, Lucknow University Village Research Project: *A Village Input-Output Study.* (A) (b)
   An on-going study of current flows and capital coefficients in a village area of central India.

5a. Delhi School of Economics, University of Delhi, *Miscellaneous Studies.* (D)
   Various prospective or on-going studies of small-scale industry and transport, the impact of particular development projects on regional investment and employment, and the pattern and magnitude of investment in India from 1900 to 1939.

6. Delhi, University of, *Study of Light-Engineering Industries.* (A) (b)

An on-going study (by Dahr) of capital coefficients and current inputs in light engineering industries in India, which will also involve a comparative treatment of similar coefficients in American industries.

7. Economic Research Institute, American University of Beirut (A. Y. Badre, Director). (D)

Various members of the faculty have established a research seminar to study concepts of capital formation and various methods of measurement which have been used in other countries. This study is to be a prelude to a consideration of the feasibility of research on capital formation in the Middle East, and an examination of the skills and costs required for its execution.

8. Gokhale Institute, *A Study of Village Money Flows.* (A) (a)

An on-going study (by Professor Dandekar) of receipts, expenditures, assets and liabilities within five villages and between these villages and the outside world.

9. Gokhale Institute, *A History of Business Organization in India.* (A) (b) (A) (b)

An on-going study (by Professor Sovani) of business organization from 1914 to 1952, dealing with the managing agencies and other forms of business control, and the shift from British to Indian ownership.

10. Harvard Research Center in Entrepreneurial History (Professors Cole, Aitken, Gershenkron, Handlin and Jenks). (A) (b)

An on-going project. Different members of the Center are working on case studies of entrepreneurship in American and Western European industries, the conditions and patterns behind the emergence of entrepreneurship in European economic history, and the role of elites in furnishing the drive behind and the personnel for the entrepreneural class. Publications include the periodical *"Explorations in Entrepreneural History"* and occasional books and papers by members of the staff.

11. Harvard University Law School, *A Comparative Study of Internal Taxation* (S. Surrey, Director) (A) (c)

An on-going study of tax systems, methods, and institutions in underdeveloped areas, with emphasis on the effect of taxation on capital formation and economic growth.

12. Indian Statistical Institute, Calcutta, *National Sample Survey.* (A) (b) (a)

An India-wide survey of physical output, and physical and monetary flows in rural and urban households, industries, etc., covering both rural and urban areas. The survey is designed to provide sectoral breakdowns for national income calculations and is the most detailed work of its kind under way, dealing with income, expenditures, savings and investment, in India.

13. Institut de Science d' Economique Appliqué, Paris. *General Research on Underdeveloped Areas* (Maurice Bye, Director) (Entire Outline)

Under the direction of Professor Maurice Bye the Institut has undertaken an investigation of theoretical research for underdeveloped countries. The orientation is broad, including definitional, economic, political, fiscal, technological and financial aspects.

14. Massachusetts Institute of Technology, Center for International Studies (M. F. Millikan, Director). *Political and Economic Development of Underdeveloped Areas.* (Entire Outline)

A comprehensive investigation of many aspects of capital formation and economic development problems more generally, focussing particularly on India, Indonesia and Italy. In particular the Center plans to study existing technologies in selected areas, in conjunction with a consideration of variable factor proportions and new technological possibilities, as a guide to the kinds of capital formation required under specific circumstances. The inter-sectoral impact of development in particular sectors of the economy will also be considered. The Center is also planning selected case studies of labor-management problems in India and their effect on productivity. These specific studies are set within the context of a generalized approach to the political and cultural, as well as economic, requirements of growth.

15. National Bureau of Economic Research. *Foreign Demand for Capital,* (Solomon Fabricant). (A) (c)

After allowing for relative price changes, private capital export from the United States during 1947 to 1952 is below the rate of the 1920's notwithstanding the fact that the United States has a larger population, higher income and a larger volume of savings than it did 25 years ago. The present study will investigate the meaning of this experience, especially in relation to the prospects for increased foreign investment by the United States in the near future.

16. Reserve Bank of India, Bombay. *Miscellaneous Studies and Research.* (D)

The Bank's research staff has various studies under way dealing with capital movements on international account, the financing of capital formation by Indian corporations, and the effect of public monetary and fiscal policies on private investment and business activities.

17. Reserve Bank of India, Bombay. *Rural Credit Survey* (to be published in 1954). (A) (b) (a)

A survey of 600 villages with more detailed investigation of a smaller sample, dealing with the sources and magnitude of credit supply, and the use of credit for capital formation and other purposes.

18. Reserve Bank of India. *Survey of Capital Formation in Joint Stock Companies.* (A) (b)

An on-going study of the balance sheets of approximately 1,000 companies estimated to represent about 85% of the total capital of all joint stock companies in the country. The survey is to focus on such questions as the rate and quantity of capital formation, and the profit position of the companies concerned.

19. STALEY, E., Director, Standard Research Institute. *A Manual on Industrialization of Underdeveloped Areas.* (A) (b)

A research study currently under way dealing with criteria and procedures for determining the economically most suitable manufacturing industries and their relative priorities in underdeveloped countries. Special attention is being given to the necessary scale of operations and the size of the market required to support reasonably efficient operations in different types of industries.

20. *The Labor Problem in Economic Development,* DUNLOP, J., HARBISON, F., KERR, C. and MEYERS, C. (A) (a) (A) (b)

A planned collaborative study, involving Harvard, M.I.T., the University of Chicago and the University of California and covering experiences in four developed countries (France, Germany, Japan and Italy) and one underdeveloped country (India). The central problem to be considered by the study is the character and adequacy of managerial responses to the emergence of a non-agricultural labor-force, and incidentally the effect of these responses on the productivity of capital.

ADDITIONAL BIBLIOGRAPHY

INTERNATIONAL ORGANIZATION PUBLICATIONS

GENERAL—*International Trade and Arrangements*

1. *1955 Survey of Primary Commodity Markets.* (Sales No. 1955. II.D.2), 122 pp., $1.75 (A-a)

2. *First Expert Working Group on Technological Centres.* (Sales No. 1955. II.H.2) Copenhagen, 10 May to 4 June 1954, 119 pp., $1.25 (D)

3. *Inter-Latin American Trade: Current Problems.* (Sales No. 1957. II.G.5) $1.25 (A-c) (D)

4. *Selected Problems of Production and Trade in the Near East.* (Food and Agriculture Organization, 1957). $1.75 (A)

GENERAL—*Capital Formation and Economic Development*

5. *Foreign Capital in Latin America.* (Sales No. 1954. II.G.4) 164 pp., $1.75 (A-c)

6. *Non-Ferrous Metals in Under-Developed Countries.* (Sales No. 1955. II.B.3) 129 pp., $1.50 (A-a)

7. *Scope and Structure of Money Economies in Tropical Africa.* (Sales No. 1955. II.C.4) 52 pp., $0.50 (A-c)

8. *Special Study on Economic Conditions in Non-Self-Governing Territories.* (Sales No. 1955. VI.B.I) 219 pp., $2.00 (Entire Outline)

118

9. *Taxes and Fiscal Policy in Under-Developed Countries* (Sales No. 1955. II.H.I.) 124 pp., $1.00 (A) (C)

10. *Per Capita National Product of Fifty-Five Countries, 1952-1954: Statistical Papers.* (Sales No. 1957. XVII.2) $0.15 (A) (D)

11. *World Energy Supplies, 1951-1954.* (Sales No. 1957. XVII.3) $1.50 (A-a)

GENERAL—*Miscellaneous*

12. *Survey of World Iron Resources: Occurrence, Appraisal and Use.* (Sales No. 1954.II.D.5) 345 pp., $3.50 (A-a)

13. *Processes and Problems of Industrialization in Underdeveloped Countries.* (Sales No. 1955. II.B.I) 152 pp., $1.50 (A) (D)

14. *Multiple-Purpose River Basin Development.* Part I. Manual of River Basin Planning. (Sales No. 1955. II.F.I) 83 pp., $0.80 (A-a, b) (D) (Flood Control Series No. 7)

15. *Analyses and Projections of Economic Development.* I. An Introduction to the Technique of Programming. (Sales No. 1955 II.G.2) 52 pp., $0.50 (D)

16. *Bibliography on Industrialization in Under-Developed Countries.* (Sales No. 1956. II.B.2) 216 pp., $2.00 (D)

17. *Progress in Land Reform: Second Report.* (Sales No. 1956, II.B.3) $2.00 (A-b)

18. *Assistance to the Needy in Less-Developed Areas.* (Sales No. 1956. IV.2) 227 pp., $1.50 (D)

19. *The World's Requirements for Energy: The Role of Nuclear Power.* (Sales No. 1956. IX.1. Volume 1) 544 pp., $8.00 (A-a)

STATISTICAL

20. *Statistics of National Income and Expenditure* (Sales No. 1957. XVII.4) $3.00 (A-c)

REGIONAL

21. *Review of Economic Activity in Africa, 1950 to 1954* (Sales No. 1955. II.C.3) 146 pp., $1.50 (A-a) (D)

22. *Economic Development in Africa, 1954-1955.* (Sales No. 1956. II.C.3) 100 pp., $1.00 (Entire outline)

23. *Economic Development in Africa, 1955-1956: Supplement to the World Economic Survey, 1956.* (Sales No. 1957. IL.C.3) $1.00 (Entire outline)

24. *Economic Developments in the Middle East, 1945-1954.* (Sales No. 1955. II.C.2) 236 pp., $2.50 (A)

25. *Mining Development in Asia and the Far East, 1954-1955.* (Sales No. 1956. II.F.4) 70 pp., $0.70 (A-a)

26. *Economic Development in the Middle East, 1954-1955.* (Sales No. 1956. II.C.2) 151 pp., $1.50 (Entire outline)

27. *Economic Development in the Middle East, 1955-1956: Supplement to the World Economic Survey, 1956.* (Sales No. 1957. II.C.2) $1.50 (Entire outline)

28. *Multiple-Purpose River Basin Development.* Part 2A. Water Resource Development in Ceylon, China, Taiwan, Japan and the Philippines. (Sales No. 1956. II.F.2) 122 pp., $1.25 (A-b) (Flood Control Series, No. 8)

29. *Multiple-Purpose River Basin Development.* Part 2B: Water Resource Development in Burma, India, Pakistan. (Sales No. 1956. II.F.8) $1.50 (A-a) (Flood Control Series, No. 11)

30. *A Study of the Iron and Steel in Latin America.* (Sales No. 1954. II.G.3) 2 volumes (A-a-1)
    Volume I. *Report on the Meeting of the Expert Group Held at Bogota in 1952.* 123 pp., $1.25
    Volume II. *Proceedings of the Expert Working Group Held at Bogota.* 449 pp., $4.50

31. *The Economic Development of Brazil.* Part II: *Analyses and Projections of Economic Development.* (Sales No. 1956 II.G.2) $2.00 (Entire outline)

32. *Lignite Resources of Asia and the Far East, Their Exploration, Exploitation, and Utilization.* (Sales No. 1957. II.F.3) $1.50 (A-a) (Mineral Resources Development Series, No. 7)

INTERNATIONAL BANK FOR RECONSTRUCTION AND DEVELOPMENT

33. *The Economic Development of British Guiana.* Johns Hopkins Press, Baltimore, 1953. 366 pp., $6.00 (Entire outline)

34. *The Economic Development of Nigeria.* Johns Hopkins Press, Baltimore, 1954. $7.50 (Entire outline)

35. *The Economic Development of Malaya.* Johns Hopkins Press, Baltimore, 1955. $7.50 (Entire outline)

36. *The Economic Development of Syria.* Johns Hopkins Press, Baltimore, 1955. 486 pp., $7.50 (Entire outline)

37. *The Economic Development of Jordan.* Johns Hopkins Press, Baltimore, 1957. 512 pp.,$7.50 (Entire outline)

PUBLICATIONS SINCE 1954

1. ABBAS, S. A., *Capital Requirements for the Development of South and South-East Asia,* New York, 1955.

2. ALLEN, G. C. and DONNITHORNE, A. G., *Western Enterprise in Far Eastern Economic Development—China and Japan,* New York, 1954.

3. BAUER, P. T. and YAMEY, B. S., *The Economics of Underdeveloped Countries,* Chicago, 1957.

4. BELSHAW, H., *Some Aspects of Economic Development in Underdeveloped Countries in Asia,* New York, 1954.

5. BHATT, V. V., "Capital Intensity of Industries: A Comparative Study of Certain Countries," *Bulletin of the Oxford University Institute of Statistics,* May, 1956.

6. BUCHANAN, N. S. and ELLIS, H. S., *Approaches to Economic Development,* New York: 20th Century Fund, 1955.

7. CHENERY, H. B., "The Application of Investment Criteria," *Quarterly Journal of Economics,* February, 1953.

8. CHENERY, H. B. and KRETSCHMER, K. S., "Resource Allocation for Economic Development," *Econometrica,* October, 1956.

9. DANDEKAR, V. M., *Use of Food Surpluses for Economic Development,* Poona, India, 1956.

10. DEEKSHIT, G. R., PATIL, R. K., and DATYE, K. R., "Capital Formation and Choice of Techniques in Underdeveloped Areas," *Indian Economic Journal,* July, 1956.

11. DHAR, P. N., "Some Aspects of Technical Progress in Small Scale Industries," *The Indian Economic Review,* February, 1956.

12. DOMAR, E. D., *Essays in the Theory of Economic Growth,* New York, 1956.

13. ECKAUS, R. S., "The Factor Proportions Problem in Underdeveloped Areas," *American Economic Review,* September, 1955.

14. ECKSTEIN, O., "Investment Criteria for Economic Development and the Theory of Intertemporal Welfare Economics," *Quarterly Journal of Economics,* February, 1957.

15. GALENSON, W. and LEIBENSTEIN, H., "Investment Criteria, Productivity, and Economic Development," *Quarterly Journal of Economics,* August, 1955.

16. HAGEN, E. E., "The Process of Economic Development," *Economic Development and Cultural Change,* April, 1957.

17. HAAVELMO, T., *A Study in the Theory of Economic Evolution,* Amsterdam, 1954.

18. HIGGINS, B., "The 'Dualistic Theory' of Underdeveloped Areas," *Economics and Finance in Indonesia,* (Djakarta) February, 1955.

19. HIGGINS, B., "Development Planning and the Economic Calculus," *Social Research,* Spring, 1956.

20. HIGGINS, B. and MALENBAUM, W., "Financing Economic Development," *International Conciliation,* March, 1955.

21. KUZNETS, S., "Quantitative Aspects of the Economic Growth of Nations, 1. Levels and Variability of Rates of Growth," *Economic Development and Cultural Change,* October, 1956.

22. KUZNETS, S., MOORE, W. E., and SPENGLER, J. J. (Eds.), *Economic Growth: Brazil, India, Japan,* Durham, N. C., 1955.

23. KUST, M. J., "Economic Development and Agricultural Surpluses," *Foreign Affairs,* October, 1956.

24. LEIBENSTEIN, H., *A Theory of Economic-Demographic Development,* Princeton, 1954.

25. LEWIS, W. A., *The Theory of Economic Growth,* Homewood, Ill., 1955.

26. MANDELBAUM, K., *The Industrialization of Backward Areas.* Institute of Statistics, Monograph No. 2, (Oxford) 1955.

27. MEIER, G. M. and BALDWIN, R. E., *Economic Development: Theory, History, Policy,* New York, 1957.

28. MEIER, Richard L., *Science and Economic Development: New Patterns of Living,* New York, 1956.

29. MYRDAL, G., *An International Economy,* New York, 1956.

30. PAAUW, D. S., "The Case for Decentralized Financing of Economic Development in Indonesia," *Far Eastern Quarterly,* November, 1955.

31. RIESMAN, D., "Some Relationships Between Technical Progress and Social Progress," *Explorations in Entrepreneurial History,* February, 1954.

32. ROSTOW, W. W., "Take-Off Into Self-sustained Growth," *Economic Journal,* March, 1956.

33. STALEY, E. *The Future of Underdeveloped Countries—Political Implications of Economic Development,* New York, 1954.

34. VAKIL, C. N. and BRAHMANAND, P. R., *Planning for an Expanding Economy: Accumulation, Employment, and Technical Progress in Underdeveloped Countries,* New York, 1956.

OTHER BIBLIOGRAPHIES ON DEVELOPMENT

1. BASTER, J., "Recent Literature on the Economic Development of Backward Areas," *Quarterly Journal of Economics,* November, 1954.

2. GOOCH, D. W., *World Land Reform: A Selective Bibliography,* Washington, D. C., 1951.

3. GILFILLAN, S. C. and STAFFORD, A. B., "Social Implications of Technical Advance: An Annotated Bibliography," *Current Sociology,* 1:211-66, 1953.

4. HAZLEWOOD, A., *The Economics of "Underdeveloped" Areas,* New York, 1954.

5. INTERNATIONAL LABOUR OFFICE LIBRARY. *Technical Assistance* (Bibliograpical Reference List 59). 1953.

6. LASKER, B., and EMBREE, J. F., *Southeast Asia: A Selected Bibliography*, New York, 1955.

7. PELZER, K., *Selected Bibliography on the Geography of Southeast Asia. Part III, Malaya*, New Haven, 1956.

8. SCHLEIFFER, H. (compiler). *Bibliography on the Economic and Political Development of Indonesia*, Cambridge, 1953.

9. STANFORD UNIVERSITY. *Bibliography on the Economic Development and Industrialization of Under-developed Areas.* 1953 (Mimeographed).

10. UNITED NATIONS. *Bibliography on the Processes and Problems of Industrialization in Under-developed Countries,* 1954.

11. UNITED NATIONS. *Bibliography on Industrialization In Under-developed Countries.* 1956.

12. UNESCO. *International Bibliography of Economics.* Vol. I and II, 1955.

13. UNITED STATES. Department of State. Division of Library and Reference Services. *Point Four, Far East: A Selected Bibliography of Studies on Economically Underdeveloped Countries.* 1951.

14. UNITED STATES. Library of Congress. *International Economic and Social Development: A Selected Background Reading List,* 1952.

THE QUESTIONNAIRE

ANALYSIS AND SUMMARY

To elicit information regarding work presently being performed or recently finished on the problems of capital formation in underdeveloped areas, a general questionnaire was prepared. A copy of the questionnaire is reproduced on pages 125-127.

The questionnaire is in the form of a check list designed primarily to guide the respondent in replying to a set of general and suggestive questions, rather than to elicit specific substantive or quantitative answers, as a means of surveying the current research relevant to the problems of this Study. This check list-questionnaire approach was conceived as an alternative, and in some instances supplement, to the interviews. In the covering letter sent to potential respondents outside the United States, the recipient, after answering the questionnaire, was requested to pass it on to other colleagues interested in research in this field. This was frequently done, so that the total recipients of the questionnaire are more than the number of questionnaires mailed.

The analytical section of this study is concerned with the capital formation process. Specifically most of the interest centers on three major aspects of the problem: (1) entrepreneurship and the demand for capital; (2) technological change; and (3) foreign investment.

The items mentioned in the questionnaire cover more than these three aspects. This was necessary because, at the onset of the study the writers had neither isolated nor defined the particular elements which now seem (to them, at least), to constitute the core of the matter. The replies, being orientated by the questionnaire, are neither so pointed nor focused as the argument in the major sections of this Study.

Copies of the check list-questionnaire were sent to all universities in the United States, where it was known that some research on the questions of capital formation in underdeveloped areas, or related problems is being carried on. In addition, questionnaires were sent to nearly all United States Embassies and Legations in Western Europe, South and Central America and the Middle East. Questionnaires were also sent to all the leading universities of Western Europe, South and Central America, the Middle East, as well as to the appropriate Ministries of the Governments of many of these countries. In some instances, copies were also sent to particular scholars who, it was known from an examination of the literature, are interested in the field in question.

In the Near East and South and Southeast Asia, an effort was made to identify and define current research by securing information from the Ford Foundation resident representatives. Some information regarding the nature of research at the American University in Beirut was so obtained, as were reports concerning the following Indian institutions: Delhi School of Economics, University of Bombay, University of Madras, Gokhale Institute, Indian Institute of Statistics and the Federal Reserve Bank of India.

In all, 200 questionnaires were sent abroad and 127 replies received. A table showing the origin of replies to the questionnaire appears on page 124. The replies to the questionnaires present an outline of research presently being undertaken. The pattern of that research deserves some comment. This Appendix will offer tentative comment, both substantive and methodological. The comment is only tentative, because the replies cannot be taken to represent an adequate report on the scholarly and technical work being done all over the world.

By and large, the unit of research of work presently undertaken by scholars in American universities in the area of economic development is geographical. Studies and investigations dealing with economic, cultural or institutional aspects of development are usually confined to particular countries or particular geographical areas of the world; e.g. Italy, Mexico, Southeast Asia or Africa. Such information and analysis should provide comparative data for most underdeveloped areas. Publication of reports, monographs, and journal articles, as well as periodic and occasional meetings of the scholars involved, may help to focus research interests on relevant problems, which will permit meaningful, comparative evaluations and analyses. The replies to the questionnaire-check list seem to suggest that regional comparative analyses, i.e. the consideration of provincial, urban, and subregional areas, in the light of their similar or differing problems and experiences in capital formation, have been somewhat neglected. Nor have questions of political organization and function been greatly stressed.

The University of Chicago and the Massachusetts Institute of Technology have undertaken the most ambitious and comprehensive studies of underdeveloped areas. The interests of each are broader than the analysis of the process of capital formation and accumulation. In addition to these schools, however, it should be noted that individual scholars, or small groups of scholars at many universities, e.g. Stanford, Columbia, Syracuse, California, Northwestern and Cornell Universities, are concerned with studying developmental processes in underdeveloped areas. In virtually every case, the scientific orientation of the researchers is not limited to strictly economic analyses, although there appears to be a tendency for the greatest interest, in most instances, to be placed upon economic aspects. Increasing recognition, in the United States especially, is being given to such interdisciplinary aspects of the development process as incentives, institutional change, social rigidities, and social structure. Comparative studies, geographical or historical, are, however, still lacking.

From a methodological point of view, a criticism of work in the United States is that emphasis on the processes of local, community or sub-regional organization and development have been slight as compared to the stress on national or broad regional development and organization. This might tend to veil significant political and social relations between a given region or city, and the government or great metropolis and its economic agencies.

It is very likely that as the research, knowledge and interest in the developmental field matures, such comparative, functional and institutional analyses will be made more often, and for more geographical and social areas. Were more comparative studies undertaken, it is possible that a series of meaningful, middle generalizations could be adduced, which ultimately would lead to major generalizations, and which would be meaningful, in themselves, for many programs of development. Middle-range generalizations are often lacking in the present phase of underdeveloped areas research. There is a tendency in some of the broader analyses to make generalizations which, supposedly having universal application, are not of great value in assisting in the understanding and solution of specific problems.

The responses from the underdeveloped areas themselves indicate a smaller concern with generalized theories of development than is true for the United States. For example, in India, Pakistan, and the Middle East, the work undertaken seems to be highly pragmatic and immediately purposive. Much work in these areas has largely been undertaken by government or semi-governmental agencies, e.g. banks. These on-the-spot studies are designed to answer specific questions raised by industrial or economic development. The lack of interest in generalization is understandable.

However, a middle ground between a unique interest in problem-solving on the one hand, and the universal approach on the other hand, would undoubtedly assist knowledge and insight into the development process to grow faster.

In general, European universities and research agencies concerned with the capital formation process in underdeveloped areas are also less concerned with general theoretical formulations or non-economic analyses than their counterparts in the United States. However, there are some notable exceptions to this, e.g. at the University of Oslo in Sweden. The best example of a limited approach probably is in the case of the German universities and research agencies. With but minor exceptions the German scholars who responded to the check list seem to have restricted their research to detailed, particular problems such as land-utilization in a particular area, or some specific international trade problem. Indeed the particularist orientation of the German research group in this field has been narrowed down in some instances to what appears to be problems of particular business firms or banks. This attitude was also reflected in the replies received from Holland. None of the Dutch universities contacted indicated that any substantial research was being done on capital formation in underdeveloped areas. Similarly the Scandinavian and Belgian universities report little research in problems of underdeveloped areas.

French scholars, on the other hand, are concerned with underdeveloped area research to a considerable extent. The *Fondation Nationale des Sciences Politiques* is offering a course of study for those interested in economic development in underdeveloped areas. Under the auspices of the *Institut de Science Economique Appliqué*, several French scholars are conducting a world inquiry connected with the problems of underdeveloped countries. The questionnaires sent out by the *Institut* group show a deep and broad understanding of the problems of economic development in underdeveloped areas.

Interest in underdeveloped areas in scholarly circles in Great Britain tends to be greater than on the Continent. In Great Britain, scholars do not seem to be primarily concerned with developing theoretical models of underdeveloped areas. Their interest, too, lies in detailed investigations of specific problems. Many of the replies received from British universities indicate that faculty members frequently spend a year or more assisting some underdeveloped area in preparation of a Government budget, or in analyzing a particular agricultural or trade problem. Particularization seems to be the general rule, although an exception is to be found in University College at Hull, where the College is preparing a general analysis of comparative economic development.

The Colonial Office of the British Government has a detailed knowledge of the university and institutional investigations in problems of underdeveloped areas. A reply from the Colonial Office, in response to the questionnaire, indicates that British experts and scholars have been used by many of the British Colonial territories and other underdeveloped areas which have political or economic connections with Great Britain.

It was indicated previously that questionnaire-check lists were sent to United States government missions abroad. The replies may be generalized into two statements:

(1) the staffs of the U.S. missions abroad are not greatly concerned with the broad theoretical questions of economic development;

(2) the many individual mission reports which relate to specific developmental problems, e.g. commodity prospects, terms of trade, private investment, etc., in specific countries, are submitted directly to the State and Commerce Departments, and in some instances are classified.

In some instances, leads to scholars and research agencies were given in the U. S. mission replies.

CONCLUSIONS

1. Concern with generalizations and the theory of the development process in underdeveloped areas is more noticeable in the United States than in Europe, although some scholars in France, Sweden and Great Britain, are working on theoretical or general aspects of the question. Partial explanations of the more specialized European approach to underdeveloped area analysis as compared to the broader. more universal U.S. approach may include the following:

(a) Europe's interest in these problems outdates that of the U.S. by many years, due to the Colonial history of many European nations. Therefore, the general concepts may be implicitly agreed upon by European administrators and scholars, while in the United States the general concepts are still being sought; and

(b) Post-World War II political and economic developments have posed international problems for the U.S. which no European country has or wants to face. Therefore the orientation of research and thought in the U.S., both scholarly and administrative, is different from the European orientation. The problems of the U.S. are viewed as global, hence the analysis tends toward universals and generalizations. The problems of Europe are specific, hence its analyses tend to be pragmatic. (A corollary of this point is more purely economic. The capital resources of the U.S. are so large, presently and potentially, that we are seeking general solutions. The opposite is true in Europe. The scarcity of capital leads Europeans to analyze specific ways and means to invest scarce resources.)

2. A geographically limited approach is widely used both in Europe and the U.S. and seems an appropriate one. It probably requires additional integrative work, not necessarily reaching for broad generalizations of universal application, but rather directed toward generalizations which apply to *types* of societies, *types* of attitudes and *comparable* situations.

3. Another approach which might profitably be followed is the comparative analysis of communities undergoing development, relating such community development to policies, attitudes and actions of the relevant power centers; i.e., banks, large scale industries or political institutions. The São Paulo experience in Brazil and the experience of particular areas in India and the Middle East deserve such analysis. (Some work with this approach appears in the literature, but none appeared in the replies to the check list.)

4. Many of the products of research are not published, but are apparently of value. Much repetitive work would be avoided if an attempt were made to bring together studies dealing with the developmental process in underdeveloped areas, and to fit the information and analyses into a series of relevant frames of reference. The plural "frames of reference" is used because it is suggested that comparative analyses aimed at less than universal generalizations are significant at this stage of our understanding. The files of the U.S. State Department and Department of Commerce are probably rich, potential sources of material for this type of classification.

5. In no instance however, did any respondent indicate any investigation of ways and means of *inducing* purposive social and institutional change. (Suppose, for example, that research indicates that family structures of types found in underdeveloped areas are such as to inhibit economic growth. If economic growth is desired by a consensus of the population in question, clearly some active social engineering is necessary with respect to achieving changes in family structures. This is but one hypothetical example of the need for this type of research.)

No report indicates that such problems or techniques of inducing or directing social change are being investigated, although by implication, many of the studies do deal with such problems, at least tangentially. This delicate phase of social process, it would seem, should be studied if the remainder of the program analyses is to be made useful. There is little point in planning for land reform, communal agriculture or factory industry if, at the same time, there is no conscious attack on the social forces which inhibit desired (or necessary) changes in customs and institutions, the lack of which threatens the success of the program. This is not the place to point out the grave implications, limitations and dangers of studies in social engineering. Let it suffice to say that they would be among the most difficult undertaken by the Social Sciences. Further comments along this line are contained in Chapter Two of the report.

NUMBER AND GEOGRAPHICAL DISTRIBUTION OF RESPONSES

	United States[1]	Great Britain	Europe	Middle East, (South and Southeast Asia)	Latin America	International Organizations	Totals
Non Government	18	14	41	6	4	3	86
Government[2]	6	2	13	8	12	----	41
					Grand Total		127

[1]United States responses supplemental to and fewer than personal interviews.
[2]No United States Government Agency in the United States was sent a questionnaire. United States Government agencies abroad were sent questionnaires; replies are included in the appropriate foreign area. In six instances, United States Agencies abroad referred the questionnaire to agencies in the United States.

The check list used is reproduced below:

CHECK LIST-QUESTIONNAIRE

Capital Formation and Foreign Investment in Underdeveloped Areas
Suggestive Check List of Research Topics

Although capital formation is not the only factor affecting economic growth, it is clearly a basic part of the problem. Economic development is directly influenced not only by the amount, but by the kinds of capital formation as well. The process by which capital formation, including the flow of capital from abroad, is set in motion in underdeveloped areas, is complex, variable and by no means fully understood. It entails social, cultural, political and legal, as well as economic factors.

The attached suggestive—and by no means all-inclusive—check list is designed to ascertain information concerning research that is underway or completed dealing with capital formation and foreign investment in underdeveloped areas. The list attempts to identify certain of the more obvious factors relating to the process of capital formation in an effort to build up an inventory of the relevant work that is going on in this field.

It is requested that the listed items to be answered by a brief statement on the nature, scope, and title of the relevant research work underway or already completed, the country or area covered, and the name or names of the individuals or organizations responsible. For the purposes of this inquiry, research work on the listed items is only of interest to the extent that it has some identifiable relationship—direct or indirect—to the needs, types, quantities and rates of capital[1] formation in underdeveloped areas.

---

[1] The term "capital" is frequently used to convey different meanings. As used in this check list, it is intended to denote primarily such real production facilities as tools, machines, transport facilities, plant, equipment, and other production facilities including value added by clearing land, new plantings of crops with long-growth periods, etc. If the researcher concerned uses the term in a different context, for example to cover investment in "human" as well as real capital through training, health, and educational outlays, this should be so indicated in answering the questionnaire.

Check List of Research on Capital Formation and Foreign Investment
in Underdeveloped Areas

A. *Economic and Related Factors as They Affect Capital Formation*
   (a) Some factors affecting the supply of capital
      1) Physical resources, factors of production, manpower and employment
      2) Prices, costs, and returns to factors of production
      3) Population trends
      4) Income, savings and consumption—national, provincial, village
   (b) Some factors affecting the demand for capital
      5) Technology, entrepreneurship, management and administration
      6) Government and private roles in capital formation—magnitudes, kinds, rates, opportunities; economic planning, development programs, etc.
      7) Capital requirements in agriculture, industry, other sectors—forms, quantities, and priorities
         (i) size of market as limitation on demand for capital
         (ii) overhead and social capital requirements
      8) Land tenure, land reform, and rural agriculture
   (c) Financial factors affecting both the demand and supply of capital
      9) Internal financial considerations
         (i) money, banking, credit (rural and urban), interest rates, capital markets
         (ii) budget policies, taxation, etc.
      10) External financial considerations
         (i) trade, balance of payments, foreign exchange reserves and commercial policy
         (ii) public loans and grants
         (iii) private foreign investment—incentives, magnitudes, barriers

B. *Social and Cultural Factors as They Affect Capital Formation*
   1) Social, cultural and religious values and patterns; the role of tradition
   2) Attitudes toward wealth, progress, investment, foreigners, etc.
   3) Family, clan, village systems and organizations
   4) Class structure

C. *Political and Legal Factors as They Affect Capital Formation*
   1) Political processes and power
   2) Internal politics and nationalism
   3) Public administration (See A (5) and (6) above)
   4) Federal and provincial powers and responsibilities
   5) Legal frame work for capital formation—barriers and incentives

D. *Other Factors as They Affect Capital Formation*

THE INTERVIEWS

FROM OCTOBER 1953 through January 1954, over 60 interviews were held in connection with this study. The interviews were with people in the United States Government, in private business and in academic institutions, who have had direct experience or have done theoretical work in connection with problems of capital formation and foreign investment in underdeveloped areas. The purpose of the interviews was to get the reactions of leading public and private administrators, scholars, business men and legislators to the problems of development.

The central ideas which arose during the course of these conversations may be summarized under four headings corresponding to the major sections of the Report. In fact, the attempt to organize the various ideas played a part in determining the structure of the Report itself.

I

Under the heading referred to in the text as "Entrepreneurship and the Demand for Capital," there was a marked consensus concerning the major importance of psychological, sociological and institutional factors. In general, the importance of these factors was conceived as operating through the stimulus or inhibition which they offer to entrepreneurship, and to their effect on both the quantity, and form of savings in underdeveloped countries. In using the term "entrepreneurship," it was clear that quite different meanings were intended by different individuals interviewed, and frequently the meaning attached to the term by a particular person changed depending on his context. Sometimes, the term was used in the Schumpeterian sense of an innovator; sometimes as a manager or administrator; and sometimes as a general symbol for a whole system of social values and cultural norms.

The emphasis placed on sociological factors was expressed in a number of different ways. For example, some of those interviewed stressed the importance of institutional barriers to investment, using the term "institution" to cover the presence or absence of such factors as credit, capital markets, and appropriate legislation, as well as the lack of growth-promoting norms of social conduct. Others expressed this emphasis in terms of the frequently encountered gap between the articulated desire for economic development and the attitudes and behavior necessary to achieve development. Still others emphasized the effect of socio-psychological factors on career preferences and economic incentives. Despite the definitional differences, there was a striking similarity in attitude and analysis among theoretical economists as well as business men and Government officials on this point.

Several of those interviewed made specific suggestions concerning either research needs or program possibilities in this broad field. A fruitful type of suggestion concerned the undertaking of case studies, both historical and current, to identify the reasons behind a successful emergence of entrepreneurship in particular areas and particular industries at various times. Other suggestions made included the following: (a) the possible role of American Schools of Business Administration in developing new curricula for use in underdeveloped countries to stimulate entrepreneur activity; (b) an analysis of the effectiveness of different kinds of foreign study programs in stimulating entrepreneurship after the student has returned to his own country; (c) an attempt to develop categories for classifying different types of societies according to their receptivity to entrepreneurial behavior and economic growth.

II

Under the heading of "Technological Alternatives and the Optimum Use of Capital," particular stress was placed on the importance of technological progress in raising productivity, quite apart from the increased quantity of capital that might be needed to introduce new methods. One economist noted that it is only likely, at best, that new investment in underdeveloped areas, apart from technological change, will yield a 10-15% return, which may be little more than is needed to keep pace with a growing population and increased consumption by capital owners. Significant economic development is likely to require yields of 6 or 7 times this amount, which implies a high rate of technological advance as well as an increase in the capital stock.

In several cases, the view was expressed that investment programming in underdeveloped countries should consider technology as something that can be adapted to suit the availability of resources in specific underdeveloped countries. While major stress was laid on the variability of capital-output and capital-labor ratios, reference was also made to the possible variability of scale and locational patterns for various kinds of industrial investment.

There was fairly general agreement concerning the need to investigate the question of technological variability, e.g. by empirically comparing the technology of different countries with respect to specific industries. There was however considerable difference among those interviewed concerning the probable results of such investigations. One view was that technical coefficients of production could only be varied within a narrow range for most industries, while another view was that the range would probably prove to be wide.

There was general endorsement of the view that the intersectoral consistency of different investments needs to be taken into explicit account in determining optimum investment decisions in economic development programming.

III

In discussing foreign investment, the view was frequently expressed that private American capital would at best play only a small role, quantitatively, in meeting the capital requirements of underdeveloped countries. Even this small role, however, implies a need to determine the specific investment opportunities which exist. In general, the business people interviewed placed greater emphasis on the specifics of investment opportunities, while the Government officials placed more emphasis on the broad question of investment "climate" in underdeveloped countries. In several cases, the possible contribution of management contracts was emphasized in place of, or in addition to, direct investment.

IV

Of the several other ideas that were advanced in the interviews, which do not fit under the above headings, two might be mentioned in particular.

First, considerable disagreement was expressed concerning the need for protectionist commercial policies in stimulating indigenous capital formation. In addition to the infant-industry argument, it was suggested that protectionism could play a particularly useful role through its effect in building up a skilled labor force, even if the particular industry in question never became competitive itself. Others interviewed expressed the contrary view that any investment stimulated by protectionist measures was likely to be a "second best" alternative, since opportunities for higher-yielding and competitive investment could be safely presumed to exist.

Second, reference was frequently made to the important bearing of the population problem on capital formation. This relationship was expressed in terms of the danger that unchecked rates of population growth might nullify any increased output resulting from new capital formation. At the same time, the need for relating estimates of capital requirements to antici- pated rates of population growth was stressed.

INSTITUTIONS AND ECONOMIC DEVELOPMENT[1]

THE PROGRAMMING OF ECONOMIC development has been largely based on theories and assumptions which place primary stress on technological change and capital formation. Related to these approaches have been the practices of surveying existing methods of production in terms of yields and productivity, and the existing size and pattern of investment through an analysis of national income and expenditure accounts. The surveys provide a logical basis for program formulation, i.e., for appraising the possibility of raising output by introducing new methods of production, and estimating the extent and kinds of new capital formation required and the increases in domestic savings or foreign capital needed to meet these capital requirements.

While inadequacies of existing technology and investment invariably characterize underdeveloped economies, these characteristics are perhaps correlative rather than causal. The inadequacy of technology and capital formation may be due less to a shortage of information about techniques or of potential savings, than to shortages of the "right" kinds of institutions—"right" implying those kinds of institutions which permit or stimulate, rather than impede, the adoption of new techniques and the formation of productive capital.[2] In other words, institutions—as well as capital and technology—are productive; or, more accurately, different

---

[1]This paper was one of the results of a research project carried on jointly by Chandler Morse of Cornell University and the author.
[2]H. Belshaw, "Economic Development in Asia," *Econ. Internaz.*, V (Nov. 1952), 848-53.

institutions have differentially productive consequences.[3] Growth-promoting institutions, without themselves adding resources to the economy —or at least by a process that is distinguishable from any resources which they directly add—may so restructure the environment in which factors of production meet that the rate at which combinations occur is accelerated.[4]

Hence, besides technological and investment surveys, as bases for programming technical assistance and capital projects, there is a need for institutional surveys and institutional programming. An organized market for monetary capital, for example, may provide potential producers with an opportunity both to maintain liquidity and realize an appreciation in their assets, and this may fundamentally alter the pattern and quantity of investment in the economy. This is the kind of catalysis that institutional programming should appraise and introduce into underdeveloped countries as a concomitant of direct attempts to program investment and technical assistance. If this approach is to be systematized, it is necessary to develop a framework for analyzing how the social context influences economic behavior. The purpose of this discussion is to make some observations and suggestions concerning such a framework, with reference to problems of development programming in the economically underdeveloped areas.

We shall use the term "institution" to refer to *organizations* and *policies,* both governmental and private.[5] This limited definition is used

[3] Cf. K. E. Boulding, *The Organizational Revolution* (New York, 1953), p. 168.

[4] The acceleration might involve *new* types of factor combinations (technological change), or an increase in those already known. In the latter case, the impact of growth-promoting institutions would result in mobilizing idle resources by overcoming the conditions of underemployment equilibrium typically characterizing underdeveloped economies.

[5] Cf. B. Malinowski, *A Scientific Theory of Culture and Other Essays* (Chapel Hill, 1944), pp. 52-54. Malinowski's concept of institution stresses and distinguishes the following components: (1) a charter, comprising the institution's objectives; (2) personnel, organized in terms of defined principles of authority and responsibility; (3) the norms or rules governing the conduct of personnel in accord with the charter; and (4) the material apparatus or equipment which the institution's personnel use. The definition we are using adds the notion of policies to the Malinowski concept of organization. For some of the many and widely variant uses of the term institution, see, among sociologists, F. Znaniecki, "Social Organizations and Institutions," in *Twentieth Century Sociology,* Gurvitch and Moore, editors (New York, 1945), p. 172 ff.; R. B. Williams, *American Society—A Sociological Interpretation* (New York, 1951), pp. 28-30; S. Winston, *Culture and Human Behavior* (New York, 1933), pp. 130-32; C. M. Panunzio, *Major Social Institutions* (New York, 1939), pp. 7-27; and among economists, see E. M. Burns, "Does Institutionalism Complement or Compete with 'Orthodox Economics'?" *Am. Econ. Rev.,* XXI (Mar. 1931), 86; J. M. Clark, "Institutional Economics," *Am. Econ. Rev.—Suppl.,* XXII (Mar. 1932), 105, and K. E. Boulding, *op. cit.,* pp. 165, 169, 252. It

in order to select those elements in the existing or potential social context which can be incorporated in institutional programs, accompanying and supplementing investment and technological programming.[6] Such programs are conceived as groups of integrated and consciously planned institutional innovations designed to stimulate those kinds of behavior by management, farmers, labor, consumers, savers, investors, and innovators which can be expected to initiate and sustain growth. The following discussion does not elaborate these kinds of behavior in detail, but assumes they can be identified.

Institutions may stimulate or impede behavior leading to economic growth by their effect on (1) the direct calculation of costs and benefits; (2) relationships between production and distribution (output and income); (3) the order, predictability and probability of economic relationships; (4) knowledge of economic opportunities; and (5) motivations and values.[7] These categories may be briefly elaborated and exemplified:

1. *The Direct Calculation of Costs and Benefits.* The simplest and most direct influence which institutions can exert on economic behavior is through their impact on costs and benefits entering into the calculations of entrepreneurs.[8]

---

is not surprising that one writer divided institutional economists into two classes: "those who refuse to define institutional economics and those whose definitions disagree," P. T. Homan, "An Appraisal of Institutional Economics," *Am. Econ. Rev., XXII* (Mar. 1932), 12.

[6] In a more extensive treatment, institutions might be regarded as sets or clusters of organizations and policies, related to each other by a dominant common purpose. Those organizations and policies which link the saver, the investor, and the entrepreneur (e.g., securities markets, banks, insurance companies, loan and savings associations, credit cooperatives, monetary policies, etc), could be considered to comprise a society's "capital-mobilizing" institution. The examples cited here generally refer to specific organizations and policies rather than related clusters.

[7] Clearly, the listed categories do not conform to traditional disciplinary lines; nor are they comparable as concerns their levels of generality or their precision. Nevertheless, they are believed to focus on significant, separable, and, at least potentially, measurable channels of influence on economic behavior which are of particular relevance to problems of economic growth.

[8] In this paper, the term "entrepreneur" is intended to denote those who make or directly affect the basic economic decisions concerning investment, employment, the scale and character of output, the adoption of new techniques, etc. This use embraces the various notions of "innovating" and "imitative" entrepreneurs which are differentiated in some of the literature. Cf. C. H. Danhof's classification in *Change and the Entrepreneur* (Cambridge, 1949), pp. 23-24. Contrary to Schumpeter's model, it may be that in underdeveloped countries there is a greater shortage of "imitators" than "innovators." Frequently, even the most retarded countries seem to have at least a sprinkling of the latter but an acute shortage of the former.

In their effect on costs and benefits, institutions may directly change cost-price relationships to the advantage of particular enterprises. The initiation and enforcement of protectionist commercial policies, which raise domestic prices of imports through the imposition of tariffs or foreign exchange taxes, are a case in point. Adoption by the Philippines of a 17 per cent foreign exchange tax in 1950 directly stimulated both domestic and foreign investment within the country.[9] The creation by Japan, after the Imperial Restoration, of institutions to subsidize and make low-interest loans to new industry also contributed to growth through their direct impact on cost-benefit calculations.[10]

A particular institutional innovation may simultaneously affect both entrepreneurial costs and benefits. The small-industries development program in Indonesia, for example, is based on the creation of local organizations, called *centrales* (or *induks*) whose purpose, aided by an initial government subsidy in personnel and equipment, is to service the needs of local entrepreneurs in specific, small industries. Services performed by the *centrales* involve both purchasing and processing of intermediate products for sale to local producers, and marketing finished output. The former service reduces entrepreneurial costs; the latter increases benefits by assuring a larger and more stable demand. While in this case the effects on costs and benefits are mutually re-enforcing, it is also possible that particular institutional changes may have offsetting effects on costs and benefits.

Institutions may affect not only the *magnitude* of costs and benefits, but the *kinds* as well. By converting a share of fixed costs into variable costs, for example, institutional innovations may have a definite impact on entrepreneurial calculations and decisions. Typically in underdeveloped areas, the uncertainty associated with business ventures tends to be high.[11] Because lower fixed costs facilitate adjustment to the unexpected, they tend to increase willingness and ability to act under uncertainty conditions. Business opportunities which involve reduced fixed costs and higher operating costs are therefore likely to be more attractive to potential entrepreneurs in underdeveloped areas than those which possess the reverse characteristics, even if the present value of the antici-

---

[9]The foreign exchange tax differed from a uniform ad valorem tariff in its economic effects in that the exchange tax applied to capital and invisible outpayments as well as imports. This may explain its important political advantage; i.e., the Philippine tax was fairly easy to remove after five years.

[10]G. C. Allen and A. G. Donnithorne, *Western Enterprise in Far Eastern Economic Development: China and Japan* (London, 1954), p. 192.

[11]See *infra*, p. 146 ff.

pated increase in operating costs equals and sometimes even if it excels the reduction in fixed costs.

In British industrialization the important role usually assigned to institutional changes which converted labor from a fixed to a variable cost provides a case in point. Economic historians have stressed the pressures increasingly exerted on the feudal serf by the manorial system in England and by the enclosure movement, as well as the attractions represented by the rise of towns, combining to stimulate a move to the towns and the creation of a wage labor force.[12] When the overhead costs of labor in the feudal manor became the "risk of existence" borne by the worker, the entrepreneur's calculations were fundamentally altered. With fixed costs lowered, and labor now a variable cost, urban investment grew rapidly. Current social legislation in underdeveloped countries may sometimes have a reverse impact. For example, Indian legislation which involves maintenance-of-employment requirements tends to make labor a fixed rather than variable cost with a corresponding influence on entrepreneurial calculations.

Institutional innovations which do not lower fixed costs may have a comparable effect on entrepreneurial calculations by making such costs easier to bear. Thus, establishment of a publicly supported market for equity capital may enable an entrepreneur to share fixed costs by sharing ownership. With this purpose in view, the government of Indonesia has recently helped to organize a stock market in Djakarta, though it is still too early to evaluate results.

Credit institutions may also facilitate the bearing of fixed costs by altering the share of initial investment requirements which can be met from the entrepreneur's future income rather than his current resources. Generally, in underdeveloped countries few institutions perform the normal function of extending long-term credit. Those which appear to do so often impose prohibitive collateral requirements and interest charges which in practice sharply restrict the access of entrepreneurs to loan funds.[13] Alternative credit facilities and policies may be a pressing, though not readily apparent, requirement for accelerated growth.

[12]M. Weber, *General Economic History* (London, 1927), pp. 128-30, and P. Mantoux, *The Industrial Revolution in the Eighteenth Century* (New York, 1927), p. 156 ff.
[13]Normally this situation might be attributed simply to the risk involved. Frequently in underdeveloped countries there may be a considerable divergence between the "objective" risk and the lender's "subjective" calculation of risk. Where the yardstick of precedent is absent, subjective risk may tend to be unduly high. Cf. H. G. Aubrey, *Industrial Enterprise in Underdeveloped Countries* (New York, 1953), pp. 14-16.

   2. Relationships Between Production and Distribution. Western technicians working in underdeveloped countries have frequently been struck by the apparently "irrational" character of individual responses to demonstrated economic opportunities. The marked and rapid impact on productivity of artificial fertilizer, row planting, double-cropping through irrigation, and other innovations in agricultural techniques, may be demonstrated without producing any perceptible impetus toward an adoption of these improved methods. Assuming the obstacle is not a shortage of capital, this inertia is generally attributed to barriers of motivation and perception. Yet it is quite possible to hypothesize circumstances under which neither a shortage of capital nor motivational or perceptual barriers exist, and find a marked reluctance to adopt widespread innovation persists. Indeed, cases of this kind may be considerably more common and significant in underdeveloped areas than those situations in which resistance to growth-producing behavior is due to motivational and perceptual obstacles.

   By their effect on the structure of rewards in a society, institutions may differentiate between those *responsible* for adopting and financing innovations, and those *benefiting* therefrom. Under such circumstances, a marked inertia to the adoption of improved methods will tend to persist despite growth-promoting motivational and perceptual patterns.[14] Where institutions operate to reduce the remuneration of a factor below its marginal productivity, individual factors with a high marginal productivity may remain unemployed, and opportunities promising a marked increase in output for new factor combinations may be neglected.

   Consider the impact of land tenure institutions on incentives to innovate. One tenure arrangement typical of the Philippines, India, Pakistan, and other countries in South and Southeast Asia, involves an organized relationship between landlord and tenant in which the tenant bears all the costs of land improvements, although he must share equally with the landlord any resulting increase in output. Before an improvement can be considered advantageous to the tenant, it must yield a gross return at least twice the improvement's cost to the tenant for the given accounting period. The effect of this situation, together with the complicating role played by credit institutions typical of this area, can be illustrated by a simple example.

---

[14]Cf. J. H. Boeke, *Economics and Economic Policy of Dual Societies* (Haarlem, 1953), pp. 33-35. See also B. H. Higgins, "Economic Development of Underdeveloped Areas: Past and Present," *Center for International Studies,* Massachusetts Institute of Technology (Cambridge, June 1954), pp. 18-19.

Assume a tenant is considering a particular capital improvement, e.g., digging and equipping a shallow ground-well whose installed cost is 100 units. Assume further he can borrow for a period of two years at an interest rate of 25 per cent per annum on the unpaid balance (a not unusual rate in Southeast Asia), and with amortization of principal divided equally between the two years. If the project is to be self-liquidating during the period of the loan, it must yield a minimum of 150 units of increased output in the first year and 125 units in the second year, because the tenant must pay half of the increased output to the landlord. Quite probably, tenure and credit institutions of this type have the effect of deterring a major share of the types of investment that, financially and technically, might otherwise be within the capacity of the cultivator.

The joint or extended family system provides another example of institutions deterring economic growth by creating discontinuities between production and distribution. The joint family, which generally characterizes the Asian area, involves a system of shared rights and obligations encompassing a large number of near and distant relatives. One characteristic of these relationships is that the individual family member receives the right of support and security from the group in return for the obligation to share his wealth to provide support and security for other members of the group. Where an individual member of the group contemplates a wealth-increasing activity, e.g., through investment in a productive asset that will yield future returns, he must bear all of the costs associated therewith. Such costs are not a levy on the group since they are not essential to the individual's support or security. However, the fruits or returns from his investment *are* subject to sharing among the other members of the extended family. Because of the differentiation between responsible and benefiting economic units, what may appear objectively to be strong incentives to invest are not subjectively so regarded by the potential entrepreneur. Under these circumstances, shortages of capital, as well as motivational and perceptual barriers, may be removed without stimulating growth because the underlying institutional obstacle persists.

We have stressed the negative or deterrent role of adverse institutions which create discontinuities between responsible and benefiting economic units. Where institutional innovations remove such discontinuities they tend to convert objectively existing, into subjectively recognized, opportunities. Altered land tenure arrangements, which exempt from sharecropping the increments in physical productivity induced by a tenant's investment or his adoption of improved techniques, may be expected to have such a generative effect even if the crop-sharing arrangements applying to the normal or base output are not changed. Actually, recent land reform proposals in the Southeast Asian countries, e.g., the Philippines, have stressed the adjustment of average, rather than marginal, crop-sharing ratios in favor of tenants. While this stress has been amply justified on grounds of equity, the stimulus to productivity would be greater if adjustment were confined to the marginal ratio. Nevertheless, it is likely that any appreciable improvement in crop-sharing ratios—whether average or marginal—will have a significant influence on agricultural incentives, investment, and productivity.

3. *Order, Predictability, and Probability.* Institutions may influence economic behavior by their effect on the amount of order in the economic environment. For our purposes, economic order may be divided into two components: (a) the predictability of the possible consequences of alternative economic actions; and (b) the probability of gain or loss associated with these consequences.

Probability refers to the *risk,* or odds on gain or loss, associated with particular actions on the assumption that their possible consequences can be foreseen. Predictability refers to the subjective confidence or certainty which the individual feels toward his risk estimates, or, more explicitly, the extent to which he feels he can make any reliable estimates at all.[15] Economic order may be said to increase when the consequences of economic action become more calculable or predictable, i.e., when individuals feel more confidence in their ability to appraise the consequences of alternative action possibilities; or when probabilities are so altered that "growth-promoting" economic actions become more frequent or likely.

The above formulation assumes that "growth-promoting" actions can be objectively determined (or agreed upon) in a country's development planning, and ranked in order of priority or intensity of expected impact (e.g., increasing investment at home rather than abroad, reducing underemployment, raising savings, etc.). Where increased economic order alters probabilities, the result will be to increase the likelihood that such actions will occur while reducing the likelihood of others.

[15]For a more detailed treatment of the effect of these factors on economic decision-making, see Aubrey, *op. cit.,* pp. 12-18; F. H. Knight, *Risk, Uncertainty and Profit* (New York, 1921), pp. 216-32; A. G. Hart, *Anticipations, Uncertainty and Dynamic Planning* (Chicago, 1940), p. 52 ff; Jacob Marschak, "Lack of Confidence," *Soc. Research,* VIII, (Feb. 1941), p. 52-53; and G. L. S. Shackle, *Expectation in Economics* (Cambridge, 1949), esp. pp. 10-19, 115-16.

The notion of probability, suggested above as a component of economic order, involves both the subjective estimation and the actuarial calculation of odds on gain or loss. Cf. Knight, *op. cit.,* pp. 223-26.

Institutions may affect one or both components of economic order. Where both are affected, the results may tend to be mutually reinforcing or offsetting. Institutions which insure against certain kinds of business risks will presumably increase the predictability of the consequences of specific economic acts. At the same time they may conceivably decrease or increase the probability of gain for any individual new investor depending, for example, on the character of competition and market structure resulting from the altered predictability conditions.

There is considerable evidence suggesting that changes in the degree of order in the economic environment played a significant role in Japanese development. A recent comparative study of Japanese and Chinese economic growth, for example, lays particular stress on the increased economic order created by Japanese policy and institutions as an explanation of the widely divergent patterns and rates of growth in Japan and China. While the Japanese government directly assisted the entrepreneur and stabilized the economic environment confronting him by creating institutions and facilities to provide credit, equipment, and foreign technical advice for new enterprise, the Chinese entrepreneur remained:

> . . . at the mercy of officialdom and subject to the arbitrary exactions of central and local authorities. Even when enlightened officials invited their cooperation in some enterprise, they hesitated because they had little confidence in the consistency of government policy.[16]

While economic order is closely related to the direct calculation of costs and benefits, the two categories are conceptually distinct. Changes in economic order either make the odds or estimates of gain or loss more calculable, or they alter the odds relating to particular actions. An owner of liquid capital in an underdeveloped country may decide to hold his assets abroad rather than to invest at home because of uncertainty concerning the possibilities of devaluation. This uncertainty may be removed by a government commitment to permit withdrawal of newly invested funds at a fixed rate of exchange. The investor, though now in a better position to predict, may continue to invest abroad because he expects a rate of return of, say, 6 per cent with a .99 chance of gain compared to a rate of return from investing at home of perhaps 8 per cent with a .66 chance of gain. A further increase in economic order might encourage

---

[16]Allen and Donnithorne, *op. cit.*, p. 192 ff. and p. 248. The arbitrary and unpredictable use of political power in France has also been stressed as a barrier to that country's early economic development. See, for example, G. Renard and G. Weulersse, *Life and Work in Modern Europe* (New York, 1926), p. 364.

domestic investment by raising the chance of gain to .90 (i.e., altering probabilities) without affecting the rate of return. By contrast, an institutional change acting directly on costs and/or benefits might also encourage investment at home by raising the rate of return to say 15 per cent without altering the chance of gain.

If one assumes the acceptance of a precise risk discount by the decision maker, the probability effect can readily be converted into a cost-benefit effect.[17] However, it is quite possible that the two effects will appeal differently to different decision makers, and that under particular circumstances differing institutional innovations are needed to produce one or both effects if the desired pattern of behavior is to be encouraged.[18]

It is probable that increased economic order is a crucial and widespread need in the currently underdeveloped areas. One example of successful institutional innovation in this field has been the establishment of the State Agricultural Marketing Board in Burma. The SAMB, which functions as a government monopoly in the purchase and export of rice, was formed to assist economic recovery by stabilizing the internal rice market. In contrast to agricultural price supports in the United States, the SAMB has kept rice prices in Burma stable since 1950 at a level substantially *below* fluctuating world prices. Rice producers have thus paid a heavy tax which has provided the country's main source of development financing. At the same time, producers have been partially compensated by improved predictability conditions in what would otherwise have been a highly volatile market. Within limits, the parallel to an insurance premium is clear. While obviously it cannot be demonstrated that recovery of production has been expedited, it is at least suggestive that cultivated rice acreage in Burma increased by 11 per cent and output by 10 per cent between the crop years 1950-51 and 1953-54.

4. *Knowledge of Economic Opportunities.* Institutions may also affect growth by removing or reducing those imperfections, frictions, and rigidities in the market which are due to imperfect knowledge concerning purchasing, production, technical, or marketing opportunities. Overcoming imperfections of knowledge in underdeveloped countries is, however, a considerably more subtle process than simply the diffusion of information. A few of the complications involved may be briefly noted.

---

[17]A particular decision maker may simply multiply the rate of return by the estimated probability coefficient in order to get an expected rate of return to compare with other similarly discounted alternatives.

[18]Cf. G. Katona, *Psychological Analysis of Economic Behavior* (New York, 1951), pp. 248-50.

It is a commonly accepted law of perception that the perceiver systematically overlooks what he considers extraneous and irrelevant.[19] The problem of influencing perception thus extends to the question of how to alter what people regard as intrinsic and relevant; that is, how to alter what social psychologists call the perceiver's "cognitive structure"—the associations, recollections, and inferences with which the perceiver connects what he actually perceives.[20] Cultivators who typically produce for their own consumption and use, rather than the market, may indeed value higher standards of personal welfare. However, they may not perceive the connection between using artificial fertilizer to raise yields of a commodity they *don't* need and obtaining a commodity of service (education, improved health, etc.) they *do* need. The availability of improved techniques may thus be overlooked as irrelevant to their "felt" needs. To influence perception, therefore, institutions frequently must not only disseminate information about techniques and opportunities, but must describe and facilitate the connection between such information and the realization of needs considered pressing by the perceiver.

For institutions to affect economic behavior by altering perception, they may have to act upon the perceiver as well as upon what is to be perceived. Even assuming that opportunities are perceived and that the probable consequences from exploiting such opportunities are valued, the economic agent may not perceive that it is his responsibility to initiate the action required to translate these opportunities into accomplishments. The problem may thus be one of altering the individual's perception of his own social role to embrace active response or "entrepreneurial" behavior, even if this only extends to the investment of his own labor.[21] This is a perhaps unnecessarily complicated formulation of the notion of "self-help" underlying technical assistance. To pursue the example previously cited, institutions must convey to the cultivator not only information concerning the techniques and results of improved

---

[19] R. B. MacCleod, "Social Psychology," in *Areas of Psych.*, F. L. Marcuse, ed. (New York, 1954), p. 201.
[20] D. Krech and R. S. Crutchfield, *Theory and Problems of Social Psychology* (New York, 1948), pp. 76-81. Morse has suggested that the social psychologist's distinction between cognition and perception has something in common with the economist's distinction between "stocks" and "flows." Thus, the "cognitive structure" may be considered to represent the "stock" of recollections and associations which gives significance to the "flow" of new perceptions. Cognition, as such, embraces the meaning and significance with which a perception is endowed, as well as the data or impression which the perception records.
[21] Cf. *ibid.*, pp. 72, 372-73 ff.

fertilizer use, but the recognition that it is the cultivator's responsibility to take advantage of and apply the improved methods himself.

The problem of perception involves the arrangement and integration, as well as the dissemination, of information. Institutions which help to establish systematic methods of cost accounting, for example, may have the effect of so altering the arrangement of already available information that perceptions and resulting behavioral patterns are markedly changed.

It is perhaps easier and more fruitful to exemplify than to define abstractly the kinds of institutions which may have the influence on perceptions and cognition we have been discussing. Boissonade, for example, refers to the importance of "journeymen's unions" in late medieval times in facilitating "the acquisition of technical instruction . . . [by] their members by organizing journeys from town to town and country to country which . . . sometimes lasted as long as five years."[22] In the 19th century and early part of the present century, Japan's intensive and deliberate efforts toward rapid industrialization, following the Meiji Restoration, adapted and elaborated this device. An organized and extensive program of foreign study for Japanese youth was consciously embarked upon to alter perceptions and accelerate the diffusion of information at home. This is a period and an experience in Japanese history that needs to be re-examined and evaluated in the light of current perceptual and motivational bottlenecks to growth in underdeveloped areas.[23] Knowles' emphasis on the importance, in 19th century Germany's development, of institutions created and supported by the state for spreading technical education and for undertaking industrial research, provides another example.[24]

A recent example can be cited in the striking success of India's Community Development Program in raising agricultural productivity during the past few years. Though using the same tools of technical assistance (e.g., demonstrations, free or subsidized distribution of seed and fertilizer, etc.) as the earlier and unsuccessful "grow-more-food" program, Community Development altered the institutional setting by organizing and training extension workers to function as residents in the rural villages. As accepted members of the community, they are able to communicate improved techniques in terms meaningful to the cultivators, to explain the relationship between proximate returns and the village's

[22]*Op. cit.*, p. 305.
[23]W. W. Lockwood, *The Economic Development of Japan* (Princeton, 1954), pp. 510-12.
[24]L. C. A. Knowles, *Economic Development in the Nineteenth Century* (London, 1932), p. 173.

"felt" needs, and to underscore the cultivator's responsibility for initiating improvements, thereby removing some of the perceptual barriers that had diminished the effectiveness of earlier technical assistance efforts at the village level.

Clearly, there is a close relationship between perception and cognition, and what we have referred to as economic order. The wider dissemination of coherent and integrated information, through extension services, market surveys, and similar institutions, may well affect the subjectively recognized predictabilities and probabilities of alternative economic choices, as well as the perception and cognition of opportunities. The distinction between the two is maintained because it suggests different channels of influence on economic behavior. In some cases, the failure to take advantage of an available opportunity may be due to the persistence of adverse predictability and probability conditions even though the opportunity may be perceived. In other cases, no predictability or probability estimates may be attempted because the opportunity is entirely overlooked by the individual as a result of its remoteness from his cognitive field.[25]

5. *Motivations and Values.* Values may be defined as individual and collective judgments (or assumptions) concerning what is desirable.[26] In "rational" human behavior, values provide the motivations which impel men to choose or avoid particular types of voluntary action.[27] Where motives differ among individuals or groups, differing action will result under otherwise identical circumstances. The backward sloping supply curve (of labor or commodities), frequently associated with "premodern" or "precapitalistic" societies,[28] is generally ascribed to the relatively high value placed on leisure by the worker or producer in these societies. Similarly, such growth-inhibiting phenomena as a highly inelastic and stable supply of entrepreneurship, widely varying wage rates for comparable labor in "native" and "western" enterprise, and varying marginal efficiencies of capital which show no tendency toward

---

[25]Krech and Crutchfield, *op. cit.,* pp. 76-77.
[26]The term "value" as used here refers to norms and standards of judgment rather than the special meaning it is accorded in economics. Cf. J. J. Spengler, "Sociological Value Theory, Economic Analyses and Economic Policy," *Am. Econ. Rev., Proceedings,* May 1953, XLIII, 342-43.
[27]Social psychologists frequently trace motivations to "needs" and "goals" rather than "values." But since values determine needs and goals, in "rational" as contrasted with "instinctive" behavior, the distinction does not appear fundamental, at least for our present purposes. Cf. MacCleod, "Social Psychology," *op. cit.,* pp. 193-97.
[28]See, for example, Boeke, *op. cit.,* p. 40.

equalization, may be explained in terms of the differing values motivating entrepreneurship, labor, and the owners of capital in underdeveloped societies.

Two points might be added to these general comments. The first concerns the ordering and weighting of values and motivations. The major difference in value and motivational patterns between developing and nondeveloping societies may lie not in the presence or absence of particular values (e.g., progress, wealth, economic security), but in the ranking and weighting of these values relative to others (e.g., status, leisure, tradition). Achieving or shaping a "growth-promoting" pattern of values and motivations is thus frequently not so much a problem of transplanting unfamiliar values as it is of reordering existing values.

Second, values may be related to one another not only hierarchically (by ordering and weighting) but also instrumentally.[29] A value X may be regarded as a means to Z, as well as something to be desired in itself. Status and prestige may motivate action (or inaction) because they are valued in themselves, and also because they are a means to the achievement of economic security. To revert to a previous example, where the member of the joint family is not only accorded prestige and status but is also provided with a certain degree of economic security by the family, there will be a stronger motivation for him to remain within the established family unit than would be the case if the second valued consequence were not linked to the first. The separation of such "linked" values may be of significance in connection with the programming of growth-promoting institutions. If, for example, it becomes possible to realize economic security in underdeveloped countries through other means than those which depend on the established status and prestige structure, the character of economic choices (e.g., career-choices, investment decisions, etc.) may be significantly affected. A further comment on this point will be made below.

What significance do these observations have with respect to the relationship between institutions and economic growth? By way of answer, it is suggested that institutions—if they are operative and effective—can modify and activate values and motivations.

In sociological literature discussing the relation between values and institutions, the causal sequence is generally presumed to be from changes in values and motivations to changes in institutions.[30] It is

[29]Cf. K. J. Arrow, *Social Choice and Individual Values* (New York, 1951), pp. 86-87; and H. A. Simon, *Administrative Behavior* (New York, 1947), pp. 49-50.
[30]Cf., for example, Williams, *op. cit.*, pp. 373-74.

therefore presumed that significant changes in the institutional structure of a society must be preceded by a major shift in the society's value
pattern. The familiar thesis attributing the growth of capitalist institutions in the West to the ethical innovations of the Protestant Reformation
is an example of this view. The hypothesis we have suggested stresses the
converse view that institutions can cause changes in values and motivations where these offer serious impediments to growth.[31] In the case cited,
it might therefore be argued that an innovation in religious institutions
led to the ethical innovations which accelerated the rise of capitalism.

In many currently underdeveloped countries, the valuational pattern
—or those aspects of the pattern which are most adverse to growth-
promoting economic behavior—may be a rationalization of an institutional structure which inhibits growth. One way of adjusting to the fact
that credit institutions charge excessive rates of interest, or that increased
earnings may produce a flood of indigent relatives with whom the increase
must be shared, is to adopt the view that, after all, increased output and
earnings are not as important as leisure and salvation. What, therefore,
appears to be a unique motivational characteristic of the "native"
economy, may actually be an expedient accommodation to adverse
institutions.[32] Under such circumstances, appropriate institutional innovations may produce a marked reordering in apparent values and motivations; that is, in the observed behavioral patterns from which values
and motivations are inferred.[33]

Institutional innovation may have a similar effect on value reordering by separating "linked" values. As previously suggested, if status and

[31]Generally speaking, it is more accurate to describe the relationship between institutions and values as *interactive* rather than causal in one direction or the other. However, the position taken in the text derives from a conviction that most current writings
on this problem in the underdeveloped areas have tended to overstress the causal pri-
macy of values at all levels, and hence to overlook the equally important influence
which institutional innovations can exert on values and motivations.
[32]Gerschenkron has expressed a somewhat similar point of view by observing that adverse values may not deter entrepreneurship (in "premodern" societies) unless these
values or attitudes are allowed to become crystallized in adverse action. A. Gerschenkron, "Social Attitudes, Entrepreneurship and Economic Development," *Explor. Entrep.
Hist.*, V (Oct. 1953) , 15.
[33]Warren E. Miller, of the University of Michigan, Ann Arbor, has suggested that even
though values originally evolved as a rationalization of an adverse institutional structure, they may be no less resistant to change. Though recognizing that my position
implies a certain humanistic determinism, I would argue that an altered institutional
structure can provide an opportunity for competing values to be perceived and adopted.
In my judgment, human experience suggests that where there is an adequate opportunity for choosing "growth-promoting" values, the human species shows a marked propensity to make such a choice. Humans tend to value economic growth provided they
have a reasonable chance to perceive it and to participate in it.

prestige are valued not only in themselves but as necessary means to economic security, the provision of alternative means to the latter goal, e.g., by insurance against unemployment or illness, may well diminish the relative value placed on status-oriented behavior.

Clearly, the inference of value reordering from behavioral changes, however persuasive they may be, is hazardous. In some cases, important changes in behavior may occur without any change in values. In India, for example, the point has frequently been made that there is a marked preference for careers in government and education rather than business enterprise or engineering. The indignity of manual labor and the relative prestige of civil service and education frequently constitute important motivations toward a pattern of career choice adverse to the manpower requirements of accelerated growth. In this case, institutional changes (affecting, perhaps, the educational curricula in secondary schools or the degree of public recognition accorded the undermanned careers) might produce significant changes in attitudes and career choice without reordering values.

Institutions may also activate values that have been operationally dormant, without reordering them. The resulting behavioral changes may be so marked as to suggest a shift in the ordering of values. In fact, the changes in behavior may be due instead to the new opportunities provided by institutional innovations for the exercise of choice according to previously dormant values, even though no reordering of values occurs. Whether the observed behavioral pattern in such cases is due to a reordering of values, or to activation of dormant values as a result of the availability of new opportunities, may be impossible—and unnecessary—to ascertain. The operationally important question is whether growth-promoting behavior, which at least by inference can be associated with a modification of values and motivations, is evoked.

We have proposed and described several categories for analyzing and evaluating the influence of institutions on economic behavior. There are obvious limitations to the approach suggested. Even assuming effective institutional innovations function in the ways suggested, the basic questions of whether, to what extent, and under what conditions "alien" institutions are transmissible remain unanswered. Certainly the inference cannot be drawn that an institution which works effectively and in identifiable ways in one social context will operate similarly, or be accepted, in a different context. The process by which new institutions come into being, and the relationship between this process and the character of the existing social structure, are not dealt with in the preceding discussion.

More specifically, the preceding discussion has dealt with the influence of institutions in partial and static terms. Interrelationships among the categories have been alluded to rather than fully discussed. Yet, clearly, the functioning of effective institutions is likely to cut across many if not all of the categories suggested.[34]

Notwithstanding these limitations, certain results may follow from the taxonomic approach described. It may provide a framework for a more systematic discussion of the relationships between institutions and economic growth than has thus far taken place. An elaboration of the approach suggested may help in the classification and comparison of existing institutions in underdeveloped countries in terms of their influence on growth. Finally, it may assist program analysts in uncovering institutional obstacles to growth and in appraising the needs of developing countries for particular programs of institutional innovation.

[34]An interesting case study illustrating this point is the recent study of the Philippine-American Life Insurance Company by the National Planning Association. The study describes the Company's striking and rapid success in redirecting existing savings, apparently increasing the average savings propensities of many middle-class families, undertaking long-term productive investments itself and stimulating other enterprises as well. In the terminology we have been using, the company's generative influence in these fields, as described in the study, has involved an identifiable impact on motivations and perceptions, as well as on the amount of order in one segment of the economic environment, and on the benefits accruing to savers from using their income in an unaccustomed way. J. Lindeman, *A Case Study of the Philippine-American Life Insurance Company* (Washington, D.C., 1954).

SCIENCE AND DEVELOPMENT

UNDERDEVELOPMENT IN AN INSTITUTIONAL SETTING

During the past seven or eight years, a seminar course in the Maxwell School at Syracuse University has dealt with various aspects of under-developed areas,[1] and has included students from most of the economically underdeveloped areas of the world. The experience and training of these people varied widely. Some were in the United States on training programs, having been assigned by their governments to study at Syracuse University. Others were public officials sent to the United States to study and gain in technical competence. A few were business people desirous of learning more about the United States and its culture. Still others were university faculty members or advanced graduate students who came to the United States, either with or without government or university support, to study at an American university. The point is that the group was diverse in background and education, but all members belonged to the educated classes of their respective countries.

During the course of the seminars the students were asked the same basic questions, in various ways. The questions in simple form are: "Why is your country less developed than you believe its potential would permit it to be?"; "What factors have retarded the economic, political, and social growth of your country?"; or, more generally, "What keeps underdeveloped areas from developing?"

Many answers were given, but virtually all the answers included the

[1] The overwhelming majority of those attending were graduate students from various underdeveloped parts of the world including Vietnam, Thailand, Turkey, Indonesia, the Philippines, Japan, Taiwan, Mexico, Korea, Puerto Rico, to mention only some.

notion that the particular, peculiar religious institutions of the student's native country are a barrier to development. The attitude of the clergy, the extent of church ownership of land, and the financial claims and requirements of the religious institutions were barriers often mentioned, in addition to the ideological barriers and superstitions fostered by the church. The unanimity of the reply was startling. Distinctions were often made between the "ideal" of the religion and its practical operation, with the former often being respectfully defended, but the latter being almost universally blamed.

A second factor which was frequently suggested as a deterrent to economic growth, although without any noticeable geographic pattern, was that the class structure or the ideology of certain classes promotes individual or élite selfishness, causes great personal and institutional nonproductive expenditures, and results in social indifference and lack of enterprise. These adverse characteristics are usually associated with the wealthy, often wealthy land owners, on the one hand, and with the poorer elements of society, i.e., "the lower classes" on the other. The middle class is often (but not always) exempted from the criticism.

In brief, the widespread feeling on the part of the students attending these seminars, a group which was sufficiently large and diverse to provide an insight into the thinking of intellectuals of the countries in question, was that the social structure, with its associated psychological attitudes on the part of the power elite and masses, motivates against economic and social growth.

The answers to the correlative question were equally interesting. Asked in a variety of ways, the question boils down to, "What determines economic growth, or what are the factors responsible for development?" It was apparent that the interpretation of history, implicitly or explicitly adhered to by these students, was largely the ready-made interpretation of economic determinism or technological determinism, in the usual class conflict-imperialistic setting. Technology determines the class structure and ideology, and the determinism is unique or at best only slightly variable. Here again, the conception of historical change or development held by the students seemed to be unrelated to their economic or social status, or their native land. The history and setting of the underdeveloped area had little differential influence on the intellectual orientation of the students.

It is as if the religions which these young people were taught as children were blamed for the social circumstances of their societies, and often a religion of automatic development and destruction of the past (Marxism) was embraced as the alternative.

That these students were vitally concerned with development is beyond question. That the official policies of their countries were to support development was also beyond doubt. It was interesting, nevertheless, that the lack of development was blamed on internal elements, which represented, insofar as the power élites were concerned, important, probably *the* important elements in governmental policy making. It was as if the students were saying that Government at one and the same time was both in favor of and indifferent to development. Much of the blame for the alleged social indifference of the upper classes was, it was argued, derived from an imitation of the ruling caste of the former ruling powers. Imperialism was a concept held in very low esteem, yet many students believed that the imperial powers had done much to better the standard of life in the former colonies. That social and personal dignity was lacking in the plans and operations of the former imperial power was genuinely and deeply felt. The nationalism of underdeveloped countries is an outgrowth of their feeling of social inferiority engendered by a colonial past.

In more matter-of-fact moments, the students readily agreed that the institutional organization of society, i.e., government, education, technology, science, to name a few institutions, and the resources of the society, all have a bearing on societal growth and development.

In their turn, students frequently asked: "Is there an analogy between the preindustrial revolutionary period of Western Europe and the situation in underdeveloped areas of today?" If an analogy between the two can be found, then it might follow that the factors which were instrumental in developing preindustrial Western Europe to its present industrial status might be important in the development of underdeveloped areas.[2]

Europe prior to, say, 1500 A.D. had elements of homogeneity which the underdeveloped areas of the world as a group do not have. The essential culture of the Christian religion was common to Western Europe. Economic organization, technology, and world outlook were much more homogeneous than those presently existing between countries of Southeastern Asia and the Middle East.

It is possible that the underdeveloped areas of the world may be grouped into categories which do have common characteristics: birth rate,

[2]In this essay we have made the heroic assumption that the world is divided into three parts: the West, the Non-West, and the Soviet sphere. The "Non-West" consists of all the areas not subject to Moscow or the rigid Communistic ideology, but also not part of the Western European culture.

religion, urbanization, capital and resource availability, skill attainment, are just a few of the criteria which might be used in a subclassification scheme. Such a taxonomic investigation done by imaginative researchers would be very instructive.

The past and the present are different. Early modern Europe had still to develop a new technology. It had yet to develop its scientific spirit and fund of scientific knowledge. Social and political organizations which were to become important often did not exist. But most of all, the science and technology of Europe, with all that they imply socially and intellectually, were still a-borning.

The underdeveloped areas of today have this technology ready made. Not only is it available to them through the literature and the educational process, but the Soviet Union, the United States, and the United Nations stand ready to provide technical assistance, and often even more than technical assistance. Technology is a resource in being for the underdeveloped world.

There is, however, another difference which is worthy of some consideration. Poets, playwrights, novelists, and social philosophers of the Western world have frequently been concerned that social and personal dislocations occur in the developing world of the West. There is wide agreement that social change is a costly process to some individuals or to whole groups of people.

The political solution suggested for social dislocation has often been "socialism" or in broader terms "social reform." It is interesting to note that the latter-day revolutionary aspects of social reform or socialism have been neither successful nor widely advocated in the Western world. Rather, in the United States as well as in Europe, recent great reforms have come about through the actions of mass democracy, especially when the mass democracy has felt its power as after the two World Wars. The social service requirements and demands of the societies of Western Europe upon their governments have been increased enormously in the 20th century. Although poor in resources, skill, and technology, and strapped for funds, the governments of underdeveloped areas, too, have, as a *sine qua non* of their very existence, attempted to provide social services which match or at least parallel the social services of the wealthier Western states.

The analogy between Western Europe in the period preceding the industrial revolution and underdeveloped areas of today also breaks down. The democratic ideal and the social ideals of the newly developed areas are well formulated, even if often mutually conflicting and contradictory. The counterpart ideals in the Western European world grew slowly and along with the social and economic development. For the less well developed world, the ideals and expectations of development are insistent political and social demands.

The observer of development may properly ask, "Can economic development occur without disrupting the traditional values and ideals and ideologies of the people in question? Is economic development consonant with values, which are accepted, or at least acceptable to the great mass of people, and their (intellectual and political) leaders?" A related question is, "Can economic development occur without the reorganization of the existing class and élite structures? Will the very people who bring about the changes in society be the people in the classes discarded and possibly even destroyed in the new society?"

General questions like these are extremely difficult but nonetheless meaningful and important to any persons concerned with problems of development.

SCIENCE AND TECHNOLOGY

As we have seen, the underdeveloped world of today is not comparable to Europe in the period preceding the industrial revolution. For better or worse, the Western world has become a standard of living model and yardstick which intrigues the Non-West. Yet the institutions, resources, and attitudes which made possible the high Western standard of living are not typically present in the Non-West. Science and the scientific method are among the missing elements in Non-Western life. Other institutions and attitudes, too, are often lacking, but our concern here is with the scientific attitude.

In the ensuing discussion we shall limit ourselves to examining some relations between physical science and technology on the one hand, and economic growth and development on the other. That technological progress and science are interdependent is axiomatic. This is not to argue that scientific knowledge must necessarily result in technological change. It is conceivable that science might be concerned only with the recording of knowledge and experience, and the findings and conceptions of research and thought need never leave the laboratory except as embodied in technical papers or monographs. This is unlikely, but it is conceivable.

The pure ideal of science lies not in its application, but rather in the acquisition of knowledge as a means of understanding Nature. This ideal forces the pure scientist to concentrate on the problem at hand, and has the effect of freeing him from any concern but the accumulation and ordering of knowledge. Political events and the "security system" have played hob with the ideal during the recent past. That "security" and intense concern with the gadgetry of application may hamper scientific research is becoming abundantly clear to the United States press, public, and politicians as the result of recent technical developments in the Soviet Union.

Technology cannot develop without scientific foundation and support. The secret of the technical success of the West lies in the application of science as opposed to the continuation of rule of thumb or the experience of the craftsman. The Western world has a tremendous resource of experiment, knowledge, theorizing, and application which joins science and technology into a continuum for economic, military, or artistic purposes. The larger the basic stock of scientific ideas and formulations, the greater the raw material out of which to develop technology.

Traditionally, and except for recent work in nuclear physics related to military matters, scientific knowledge was available to all, through the free publications of findings. Only specific applications are protected by patents, and even such legal protections are not permanent. Communication among scientists is crucial, for only by communication can scientists learn of each other's successes or failures, and develop an institutional spirit which is vital in any great undertaking. With the availability of capital, a high level of income and wealth, and the virtually limitless expectation of further increases in income and wealth (conditions found in the American scene), the greater the likelihood that the stock of scientific ideas will be transmuted into practical, applied techniques and specific capital.

The transmutation of science to technology presupposes not only the availability of capital and the desire for more income, but it also requires an institutional and ideological framework which is congenial to economic expansion; in brief, it requires entrepreneurship and a class of technicians both of which understand the results of science and can manipulate them. That this process is antithetical to the growth of spiritual and nonmaterial qualities of life is not proved, and probably is not true. A spiritual life is spurious if it grows from seeds of ignorance sprouting in the soil of poverty. A spiritual life must be based on the mystical view of Nature. Superstition and magic have little in common with the mystical view of Nature. Physical discomfort as a prelude to mystical experience is not related to endemic starvation and ignorance.

The institution of science in the West is almost sacrosanct. Scientists have not been immune to popular criticism, but Science, as an institution, is treated with a veneration and respect usually reserved for the Church. Indeed in a sense the scientist has become a member of a priestly caste in the West, and is often unconsciously assumed to be able to control Nature. With a perfectly straight face Americans speak of "miracle" drugs and the "miracle" of television, yet the very essence of the word "miracle" is opposed to the assumptions of science and the faith of scientists.

By and large, most scientists of the West have refrained from building great cosmic systems. Rather, they are usually content to narrow their fields of interest to the discovery of particular relationships. Induction has been the rule in modern science for the past five hundred years. Yet induction—the recording of specific relationships—has not satisfied the scientific mind in the Western world. Observation is related to hypothesis, and hypothesis to the theoretical conception of the nature of the world or of the general class of phenomena being studied. Hypotheses which cannot be verified or theories which do not match the facts are discarded, and new attempts at generalization are made. The process of generalization or theorizing only rarely is cosmic or universal in scope. "Middle" generalizations rather than total generalizations are customary. Cosmological theorizing among scientists occurs but rarely, and then is named "philosophy" to put it into another universe of discourse.

The future as it unfolds may (and no doubt will) change our knowledge, but it is not likely to change our general conception of the nature of Nature.

The testing of idea against fact is essentially the scientific way of looking at the world and has affected the religious and general educational thought of the Western world. The introduction of the adjustment and readjustment process of scientific generalization to the field of ideals and morality has not been without pain. Some moralists have argued that value systems relate to particular circumstances of time and place, and have no absolute or general validity. This ethical relativism, has both historically and presently caused deep concern to many Western thinkers, and has given rise to a lively discussion in both scientific and philosophical circles.

The effects of scientific theorizing on religion, ethics, social science, and all other branches of human thought have been very great. The Darwinian concept of evolution has had a profound effect on all the social sciences, while the methodology of 19th and 20th-century physics has been widely adopted and imitated by the social sciences, economic theory above all. Nuclear fission and fusion will probably, in their turn, have a great effect on future Western thought.

It should not be concluded that the method of the physical sciences has enabled (or will enable) all facets of life to be explained by mechanical "laws" or "propositions." What it does mean is that the faith of the physical scientist in the orderliness of Nature has provided a base from which the method and methodology of the nonphysical sciences may operate.

SCIENCE IN THE WEST AND NON-WEST

It is difficult and dangerous to generalize about the entire Non-Western world, for it is a world of great heterogeneity. Bearing in mind, however, that what we say is not valid in every single instance, we can make certain general comments.

In the Orient, much attention has been given to the nature of things in their emotional, esthetic, and sensory immediacy. Fact, as apprehended by the senses, is treated as reality (or as irrelevance) rather than the raw material of the process which the scientific West views as the relevant generalization. To the Non-West the world of nature is often a series of unchanging, static relations. Thus, carried over to social life traditional behavior becomes necessary and moral behavior. Theoretical generalization about the physical world and the view of Nature as a process, which is the essence of scientific activity, is not generally part of the world view of the Non-West. Generalization or synthesis is reserved usually for art, manners, or religion. Nirvana is a generalization which denies rather than explains the physical (sensory) world.

The logical, orderly, mechanical process of Nature as an assumption does not exist as a general institution outside of Western thought. Yet without such a view of Nature, a technology cannot develop, for science, the root of technology, cannot exist without the assumption of orderly process. Furthermore, a view of the world as static rather than as process, as the Western science views the world, gives neither the untutored nor the sophisticated mind the capacity to recognize the need for or possibility of institutional change. A rigid moral or legal system is not necessarily a liability if a society is not changing, but when changes are introduced forcibly or through economic and political growth, conflicts between the old mores or old moral values, and the requirements of the new economy or a new body politic are bound to arise, and are bound to have serious repercussions both on individual thought and upon the relations between and among individuals and classes of people.

The Islamic civilization, up to about the 13th or 14th centuries, followed a philosophical and scientific path which might easily have been extended to parallel the later developments of the West. Greek thought and indigenous Islamic scientific curiosity were the basis of a world view which impelled great social development and economic growth. But attitudes and interests changed, and Islam's great interests shifted elsewhere. The type of world in which science is a keystone of thought and action was limited to the West, until the most recent times. In the Non-Western world, life seems to be perceived and apprehended in discrete parts. Orderliness is to be found only in some ultimate synthesis on a "high" or distant level dealing with spiritual ultimates rather than experience. This is essentially a mystical or esthetic concept, which was not unknown to the early Christian mystics.

Strangely enough, a complex society can support contradictory views without seemingly feeling any strain. Indeed, greater complexity seems to make possible greater contradiction. Religion of a mystical variety can exist side by side with a scientific orientation. Some people are attracted to one, others to the other, while still other people seemed concerned with neither or both.

There are ideological contradictions in all people. Never does one find a totally dedicated man who gives his whole interest to a single world view. Never does one find a totally dedicated society. The many-faceted nature of society eases, to be sure, the introduction of a scientific ideology into a world where it is but little known. What is needed, however, for development is a cadre of scientists, men who live in and understand the scientific world, who are allowed to work free of restraint by the ideologues of mysticism and the religious institutions. Science cannot flourish if it cannot exist. Technology cannot develop if science is outlawed.

EDUCATION AS COMMUNICATION

From the viewpoint of educational policy and program, the meaning of the preceding discussion is that the Non-Western world has a different intellectual heritage, point of view, and set of expectations from the West, the United States in particular. The major teaching enterprise of the United States, of course, is essentially directed toward training and educating its own. Forgetting for the moment language barriers and similar difficulties, the foreign student of the Non-West is likely often to be confused by the subject matter, implied assumptions, and general approach of the courses he studies in the United States.

By a great expenditure of effort, our Non-Western student may master a technical course, e.g., marketing or budgeting, but the inner meaning and setting of the technical material in its cultural milieu are likely to be missed. Nor is it clear that the mastered technique is appropriate for the society in which our foreign student will apply it. Lack of social or philosophical relevance and technical inappropriateness will frustrate the most ambitious and well-intentioned educational effort.

In this discussion we will not analyze the relations of science to society. At best we can only discuss the problem so as to expose one slight corner of its ramifications in the area of teaching about economic development.

At an operational level, the components of teaching are:

1. the teacher
2. the teaching materials
3. the techniques of teaching
4. the student.

The teacher, his techniques, and his materials, to be effective, must each be directed toward educating (influencing or changing) the student. The teacher, trained in the marketing methods of urban, high income culture in the United States, armed with cases and texts, and using a persuasive manner, may influence a Non-Western student. At best, however, the application of what has been learned has only slight relevance to an underdeveloped area. Furthermore, it is to be doubted, on a priori grounds that the teacher, artful in teaching the Western student, can always (or perhaps usually) teach the Non-Westerner with the same success if the same techniques are used.

First and foremost, it would seem that the teacher to be successful, must reorient his knowledge and technique to suit the background, needs, and orientation of the student. This is a tall order, but not an impossible one. Just as Anna taught in Siam, so can Professor Jones teach the Thailander studying in the United States, especially if both student and teacher take the time and effort to attempt more than superficial communication. This vital area of educational development needs investigation and analysis.

Such educational analysis and investigation implies developing a body of knowledge available to the teacher about the nature and changes of the world of his student. Also involved is the development of information and expectations about the social, scientific, business, and political changes implicit in development in the underdeveloped country in question. Of course, it is assumed that the teacher is intimately aware of the theory and the practices of the West.

Recent interest has centered on the training of entrepreneurs in underdeveloped areas.[3] This interest has imaginatively suggested that the entrepreneurial functions of risk taking, innovation, programming, and

[3] See p. 32, 33 *supra*.

planning can be performed both within and outside government. Where and how the functions are performed, of course, depend upon the institutional organization and process of change in the institutional patterns and relations. The problems of entrepreneurial training and development for the Non-Western world scarcely have a counterpart in the West. Yet, the entrepreneurial function is only one of many which interests or should interest the educational innovator. The role of governmental and nongovernmental administrators and administration, the skills required of business and government technicians, capital markets and banking institutions, planning and programming, administration, these are but a few examples of specific educational subject matter which cannot be faced without study, thought, investigation, and analysis.

An important service for a student from a society which desires development would be to acquaint him with the preconceptions of Western society. Not that Western society and its preconceptions should or will be the model for a new, developing society. But to train a student in technical or operational skills, or to explain a social process without providing a setting for the teaching, is poor teaching for it leads to ineffectual learning. Furthermore, the exposure to the preconceptions of the Western system will likely lead to the formulation of a more reasonable and meaningful view of society by both teacher and student.

Few teachers feel that they have mastered all the facets and ramifications of their subject. Only those with a limited intellectual curiosity would feel they have completely mastered their subject. To train students to live in a new world is a great challenge, even to a profession which faces challenges as a routine. These new challenges, however, require new knowledge and new techniques. Such knowledge and techniques must be perfected before the teaching process can become even moderately effective. As complete as the existing literature is, it probably requires reorganization and additions to be useful in a program for educating students from the less developed areas of the world.

The teaching and learning processes are part of the greater social process. The social process of the Western world, it is argued, places a great reliance (whether conscious or unconscious) on science, for science is the basis of technology, which is so important to the West. To teach technology without stressing the role of science and scientific generalization is not likely to provide a satisfactory teaching-learning relation. Nor can the process of development be divorced from science, any more than it can be divorced from other institutional structures or social attitudes. The economic growth of the Non-West is part of a more general social process.

How to teach the scientific method and outlook in addition to more substantive matters to future teachers, government officials, and businessmen concerned with development is an intriguing question. Economic theory, because of its methodological affinity to the physical sciences (especially Newtonian physics) is an opening wedge. The interrelations of the social and economic processes, the understanding of the essential oneness of the social world must be brought home to the student. It is not easy for a person who is living in two worlds to see them as really one world in transition.

The challenge to both teacher and student is to see the developing world as a process with specific content rather than as the scene of discrete, unrelated, general static relations.[4]

[4]Among the writings which have been most stimulating in the general area discussed in this section is the following list of ten. These writings, of course, do not represent a complete bibliography in any sense.

ARNOLD, Sir Thomas and GUILLANE, Alfred (eds.) . *The Legacy of Islam,* Oxford University Press, 1931.

BROWN, Donald McK. *The White Umbrella,* University of California Press, Berkeley and Los Angeles, 1953.

HAGEN, Everett E. "The Process of Economic Development," *Economic Development and Cultural Change* (Research Center in Economic Development and Cultural Change, University of Chicago) , Vol. V., No. 3, April, 1957.

HSU, Francis. "Cultural Factors in Economic Development," *Economic Development: Principles and Patterns.* Edited by Williamson and Buttsick, Prentice-Hall, New York, 1954.

MANNHEIM, Karl. *Man and Society in an Age of Reconstruction,* Harcourt, Brace and Company, New York, 1940.

MURDEN, Forrest D. *Underdeveloped Lands: Revolution of Rising Expectations,* Foreign Policy Association, Headline Series No. 119, New York, s/o 1956.

NORTHROP, F. S. C. *The Meeting of East and West,* The Macmillan Company, New York, 1946.

SOROKIN, Pitirim A. *Social Philosophies of an Age of Crisis,* Beacon Press, Boston, 1950.

WHITEHEAD, Alfred North. *Adventures of Ideas,* The Macmillan Company, New York, 1933.

WHITEHEAD, Alfred North. *Essays in Science and Philosophy,* Philosophical Library, New York, 1948.

168 *Capital Formation and Foreign Investment*

INDEX